BUSINESS
FOR PUNKS

BUSINESS FOR PUNKS
BREAK ALL THE RULES –
THE BREWDOG WAY

JAMES WATT

PORTFOLIO
PENGUIN

PORTFOLIO PENGUIN

UK | USA | Canada | Ireland | Australia
India | New Zealand | South Africa

Portfolio Penguin is part of the Penguin Random House group of companies
whose addresses can be found at global.penguinrandomhouse.com.

First published by Portfolio 2015
This edition published 2016

001

Front cover design by Rob Mackay
Design by Hampton Associates
Printed in China by C&C

A CIP catalogue record for this book is available from the British Library

ISBN: 978-0-241-29011-8

www.greenpenguin.co.uk

Penguin Random House is committed to a
sustainable future for our business, our readers
and our planet. This book is made from Forest
Stewardship Council® certified paper.

*'If we will disbelieve everything,
because we cannot certainly know all things,
we shall do much what as wisely as he who
would not use his legs, but sit still and perish,
because he had no wings to fly.'*

John Locke (philosophy punk)

CONTENTS:
INGREDIENTS FOR A BUSINESS REVOLUTION

PROLOGUE:
HELLO, LET'S CHANGE THE WORLD

'To me, punk is about being an individual and going against the grain.'
Johnny Ramone (archetype punk)

'I always said punk was an attitude . . . It was all about destruction, and the creative potential within that.'
Malcolm McLaren (original punk)

In the 1970s punk rock changed the world. It was more than just music. It was a cultural phenomenon. At BrewDog our business is built on the punk mentality. At its core punk is about learning the skills you need to do things on your own terms. At BrewDog we reject the status quo, we are passionate, we don't give a damn and we always do something which is true to ourselves. Our approach has been anti-authoritarian and non-conformist from the word go.

Completely inspired by everything punk, we set out to offer a modern-day rebellion against tasteless mass-market beers as well as a hard-core revolt against brands which are so bland they melt into oblivion. We took an anarchic, DIY, decidedly reckless approach as we tore up the business rule book and did things on our own terms. The results have been electrifying.

Rewind to 2007. Based in a shed, on a remote and godforsaken industrial estate in the north-east of Scotland, BrewDog came howling into the world. Martin Dickie (my best friend) and I set up one tiny brewery with one very big mission: to revolutionize the beer industry in the UK and completely redefine British beer-drinking culture. This book documents the philosophy that has driven our wild roller coaster, which has seen BrewDog become a cataclysmic catalyst for the craft-beer movement in the UK and beyond.

Before founding BrewDog, having turned my back on my legal career, I cut my teeth on the high seas of the stormy North Atlantic, starting on the deck of a deep-sea trawler and eventually becoming a fully qualified captain. Spending five years working in one of the toughest environments on earth and learning to become a captain taught me so much about people, leadership, teamwork and adversity. It was incredibly tough but I loved every second of it. Ultimately for a crew to be effective leadership needs to come from the top down, the bottom up and everywhere in between.

Many of my unorthodox business strategies that put wind into the sails of the pirate ship that is BrewDog were forged on the tempestuous Atlantic Ocean. In one of the most dangerous jobs on the planet there is no place for doubt; risk is all encompassing, leadership needs to be quick as well as decisive, and survival is always the first step to success. Hanging up my captain's hat was tough, but I had found something I loved even more than the ocean: craft beer.

I had always been passionate about beer and began home brewing with a vengeance in 2004 as Martin and I brewed up a storm in our garage. A chance meeting with legendary beer writer Michael Jackson led to Martin and I deciding to take the plunge, follow our dreams and start our very own craft brewery. Michael, upon tasting one of our home-brewed concoctions, told us to quit our jobs and start brewing beer. It was the last bit of advice we ever listened to.

Over the last four years BrewDog has officially been the fastest growing food and drinks producer in the UK and simultaneously the fastest growing bar and restaurant operator, topping the growth charts in not just one but two industry sectors as business has gone from strength to strength both domestically and internationally. Our business, which started with only £30,000, now has a turnover in excess of £50m and has been solidly profitable every single year since our inception.

WE TORE UP THE BUSINESS RULE BOOK AND DID THINGS ON OUR OWN TERMS.

What started in 2007 with two humans and one dog has, in less than eight years, grown organically to a business which employs over 500 people. We now ship our BrewDog beers to over fifty countries all around the world as we look to challenge people's perceptions of what beer is, and ultimately make other people as passionate about great craft beer as we put the flavour and craftsmanship back into people's beer glasses. Martin and I also host the longest running beer show in TV history with *BrewDogs* now being aired in over twenty countries.

Our brewery, still in the north-east of Scotland, is one of the most technologically advanced and environmentally friendly in the world. In addition to our state-of-the-art brewery we now own and operate over forty BrewDog craft-beer bars in flagship locations in Tokyo, London, Edinburgh, São Paulo, Rome, Barcelona, Helsinki, Berlin and Stockholm. And we have just started building a flagship brewery in Columbus, Ohio.

Starting an ambitious small business with next to no capital is gritty, intense and encapsulating. Our blissful naivety and lack of experience proved to be our strongest suit. We did not know how things were meant to be done so we just went ahead and did them in our own way. Inadvertently creating a whole new approach to business along the way.

Business for Punks outlines this revolutionary philosophy and elaborates on the good, the bad and the ugly of learning how to run and grow a company the hard way.

The small-business landscape has changed radically over the last few years. *Business for Punks* is a manifesto for a twenty-first-century business. Rip up those stuffy old text books, reject the status quo, tear down the establishment and embrace the dawn of a new era.

Keep on rocking in the free world.

James, Aberdeen, 2015

SECTION A:
STARTING A BUSINESS FOR VAGABOND VIGILANTES

The overwhelming likelihood is that your business will fail. The cards are stacked against you. Eighty per cent of new businesses fail in their first eighteen months. That's 800 out of 1,000, 8 out of 10, 4 out of 5 start-ups, which crash and burn upon launch. Fact. No matter how you write it, it's not a pretty read. This staggering mortality statistic is a stark reminder of today's brutal commercial environment. So if you're thinking of starting a business, the chances are it will fail. And it's not just your business that will get a good and proper kicking – your future, your confidence, your dreams, and of course your bank balance, are all going down with the good ship *Failure*.

Let's say you're one of the tough ones and you make it through the first eighteen months. The chance of becoming a sustainable long-term business is still less than 1 in 20. Another clarion wake-up call.

With only a 5% chance of survival you better make damn sure you're focused, ruthless, driven and motivated from day one. Then maybe, just maybe, you'll make it.

The decisions you make during your business's formative months will define your place in the world. They will be the most monumental decisions you will ever make, shaping your fledgling business in ways you cannot yet imagine. So you'd better buckle up, hold tight and step up to the challenge. You will need to make sure your ideas, and their realization, are nothing short of awesome. It is a chilling paradox that the decisions you make when things are at their toughest and you are at your greenest are ones you are going to have to live with for years to come.

You need to earn the right to exist and find a reason to be even remotely relevant. Brace yourself for the grittiest, toughest and most intense few years of your life. You'll need to be multifaceted, learning to do, and doing, everything. And you'll need to learn how to cope with rejection after rejection, learn to love being relentlessly kicked in the teeth and you'll need to revel in finding opportunities in the bleakest of adversities.

Starting your business will be savagely brutal and yet somehow enjoyable and fulfilling. This section is about laying the foundations, nailing the groundwork and ensuring the decisions you make during those very early days will stand you in good stead and help ensure your start-up will only blow up in a positive way. The rest of the book will build on the fundamentals outlined in this section.

Time to move upstream and test your mettle.

IF YOU'RE

THINKING

OF STARTING A

BUSINESS,

THE OVERWHELMING

LIKELIHOOD

IS THAT IT WILL

FAIL.

DON'T START A BUSINESS, START A CRUSADE

Businesses fail. Businesses die. Businesses fade into oblivion.

Revolutions never die.

So start a revolution, not a business.

It is no longer enough just to start a business. You need a clear purpose, a mission, and a reason for existing. Martin and I did not just start a brewery – we set out on a mission to make other people as passionate about great beer as we are. This promise and premise underpins every single thing we do and acts as a resolute reference point for every single decision we make.

Whatever type of business you start, it is your responsibility to ensure it is anchored by a strong, eminent, readily comprehensible and entirely encapsulating mission. For example:

* **Zappos did not start an online shoe business.** They started a crusade to elevate customer service through treating their staff amazingly well.
* **Noma did not start a restaurant.** They embarked on a mission to reinvigorate Nordic cuisine, complete with their own Nordic Cuisine Manifesto.
* **Apple did not start a computer business.** Their mission was to change the world through technology.

Having a mission enables everything you do to be placed in the context of a higher meaning and aligns everyone within your business towards a common goal.

Your mission needs to be singular and compelling. Your team and prospective customers need to be able to buy into it. It is your mission that will set you apart. Your biggest challenge from day one is to give people a reason to care, and that reason has got to be your mission. In today's saturated reality the market for yet another brand, another business, another product or another service, is pretty much non-existent. Yet the market for something to believe in is infinite. You need to give people something to believe in.

You need to ensure you are starting a business for the right reasons. If you just want to make money and be a big shot, go join a desperate corporate. Sell your soul to the devil and be yet another rat-race contestant in an expensive suit. Start-ups are incredibly tough environments and you will need something to sustain you. And the thing that will sustain you and your team is your mission. If money is your motivation then you need to be the greediest, meanest son of a bitch on the planet to make a business work. Solely money-focused businesses do exist, but I don't like being around them or their people. As customer savviness increases, purely money-focused businesses will go the same way as the dinosaurs. Good riddance. If your main reasons for starting a business are financial, please stop reading this book now.

Do something you love and have a clear mission. The tighter everything revolves around your raison d'être, the more your offering will resonate with customers, and the easier it will be to turn customers into fans.

Assume no one will care, assume no one will give a damn, assume no one will want to listen. Then figure out how to make people want to care about what you do. If you can't, then your business is doomed.

- **Don't just start a bakery in Idaho.** Start a crusade to educate people about the health and taste benefits of fresh small-batch sourdough bread.

- **Don't just start a hairdresser's in Berlin.** Start a quest to see how much fun it is possible for a customer to have whilst getting their hair cut.

- **Don't just start a mechanic's in Manchester.** Start a mission to redefine people's expectations when it comes to customer service in auto-care.

You have to stand for something over and above your core competency to have any chance of standing out.

People no longer just want to buy a product or service. Twenty-first-century consumers increasingly want to align themselves with companies and organizations whose missions and beliefs are compatible with, and enhance, their own belief systems. Your customers will need to be actively complicit in helping you to succeed and you need to give them a compelling reason to do so. You can make people care and make them evangelize by having a strong mission.

Having a captivating crusade at the heart of your business is the first step to ensuring your business sticks around for long enough to make an impact.

BE A SELFISH BASTARD AND IGNORE ADVICE

I love ignoring advice as much as every stupid muppet loves giving it to me. My advice, to those seeking advice, is don't even bother. Advice is for freaks and clowns. The thing about being driven is you need to know your own way.

Inevitably when you start a business, everyone you know, and everyone you don't, is suddenly an all-conquering expert. Ignore them. Stick to your vision, make your own rules and kick ass. You know where you're going and how you get there is up to you. Fie on those hammerhead know-it-all philistines; they know nothing. Other people don't understand, and they certainly don't care as much as you do.

If your business stands or falls, it should do so through your decisions, not those of any faux part-time amateur business guru. These phoney practitioners will advise you to 'Learn from your mistakes'. Learning from mistakes is for losers. Trying to find solace in the fact that mistakes may somehow teach you something is stupid logic used by lesser mortals to try to justify their own inadequacies. The only thing you learn from mistakes is that you are not good enough and that you need to get better. You need to realize that what you actually learn from are your successes.

If mistakes do get made, the key thing is not wasting time by looking to learn anything from them but being smart enough and fast enough to fix them as soon as you can. You need to be in tune with your business to spot any potential issues developing and nip them in the bud before they grow arms and legs. And by arms I mean a fully loaded AK-47 pointed at your neck.

Doing things your way sure as hell won't be easy. But ultimately it will pay off and you can revel in the fact you proved those mothers wrong.

Believe. The stronger your belief in your idea, the less need there is for others to input. The better your idea, the less credible anyone else's input will be. You know your world, you've lived with this idea, nurtured it and now you, and you alone, will make it happen. A patchwork quilt of other people's half-baked ideas and input is a recipe for nothing but disaster. Don't follow when you can lead.

Be a selfish bastard. Seriously, you have to be. If you're not 110% up for it, no one else is going to give a damn. So dance to your own tune and do it your way. Make crafted products you love, create environments you want to hang out in and give the kind of service you'd love to receive yourself.

Being obsessive, tunnel-visioned and totally focused might not make you pin-up of the month. But it will make the difference between success and failure. Your greatest asset is yourself and your unwavering belief and commitment to your business.

As well as ignoring advice, you also need to be completely oblivious to the real world. The real world is not a place but merely an excuse. A vindication of mediocrity. A justification for not even trying. It applauds the average and it sets the bar at the same height for all. Ignore it. Give it both barrels. To you it is dead. Cause of death – *its own ineptitude.*

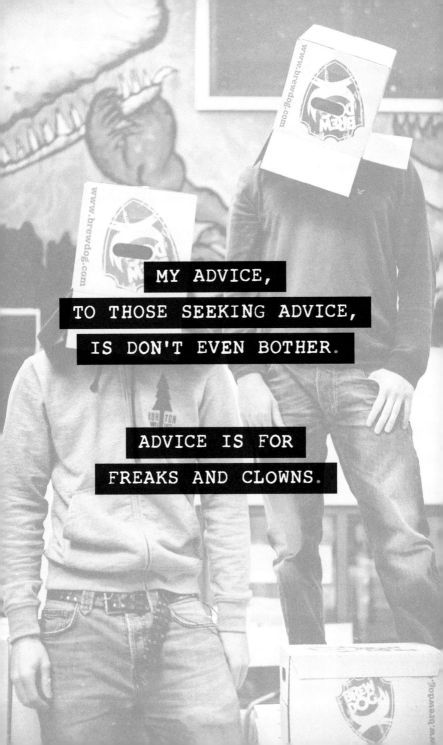

MY ADVICE,
TO THOSE SEEKING ADVICE,
IS DON'T EVEN BOTHER.

ADVICE IS FOR
FREAKS AND CLOWNS.

BE PART OF A PACK

Pack mentality rules in business. Running with an elite pack means you get there quicker and you share the pain along the way. Being part of a crack team sharpens your focus, helps you deliver and makes the journey more fun. It's a dog-eat-dog world out there, make sure you pick the right sled team to drive you forward.

A co-founding pup will make you faster, better and sharper. Being accountable to someone other than yourself is critical to sustained awesomeness. By flying solo you will also take all the fun of an epic shared journey out of the equation too.

The business landscape is ruthless, and being an only child puts you at an immediate disadvantage. Find a partner or two to share the burden with and to diversify your company's skill base. Start to build roles and structure, and your business will grow much faster. Just make sure whoever you get into bed with shares your mission and passion for hard work. Finding out they're a lazy two-bit hobo later is too late. And the fallout will be nuclear. Choose a business partner as wisely as you would choose a spouse.

Adobe, Apple, Cisco, Garmin, Intel, Microsoft and Canon are all massively successful international icons and each one was founded by at least two entrepreneurs. The odds against any start-up making it are tough; if that start-up has a single founder the odds are exponentially tougher.

If BrewDog had been a single-founder company, it certainly would not be where it is today. BrewDog has only been able to grow as quickly as it has because Martin and I were able to divide and conquer as we executed our plans to turbocharge our growth.

BREWDOG HAS ONLY BEEN ABLE TO GROW AS QUICKLY AS IT HAS BECAUSE MARTIN AND I WERE ABLE TO DIVIDE AND CONQUER AS WE EXECUTED OUR PLANS TO TURBOCHARGE OUR GROWTH.

We were able to share the workload and share the journey. Our relationship and levels of trust meant we could each focus on our respective parts of the business, secure in the knowledge that there was someone just as passionate, dogged, committed and determined working on the other parts.

Hunt in packs. Lone wolves don't feast on many jackrabbits. Build a tight and cohesive founding team and you can really put a dent in the world.

BAKE YOUR OWN GODDAMN PIE

If anyone ever tells you to look for a gap in the market, tell them to go to hell. Why anyone would want to do something that stupid is beyond me. The illusive gap that we should all apparently plug is a quick-fire route to nowhere.

The whole gap-in-the-market approach is an outdated fallacy that should be burnt and banished from history. It was probably thought up by a 'business' academic who has never even started a stamp-collecting club, never mind a business.

Don't look for gaps in the market. Don't be a pathetic leech scrambling around for crumbs off someone else's second-rate pie. Bake your own goddamn pie. Look to create a whole new market. Start a category, not a business. Be a fish in a tiny self-built pond, then grow that pond. If you swim in someone else's pond, you will just get gobbled up.

You have to narrow your focus to such an extent that there is no current market for what you are about to do. This gives you the amazing opportunity to create a whole new category. Then you can focus on growing the category rather than just differentiating your brand from the others. To be credible, your reason to exist needs to extend beyond your own brand, and a focus on growing a brand-new emerging category you are passionate about instantly gives you wider credibility and relevance. We are not about growing BrewDog, we are about getting more people to drink great beer. Period.

GoPro did not just make a video camera. They did not look for a gap in the existing camera market. They did not want to offer existing camera customers something slightly better than they already had. They wanted to sell a new type of camera to a completely new audience. They created a whole new category and pioneered tiny HD cameras for extreme sports enthusiasts and built an amazing business in the process.

The power of any brand is inversely proportional to its scope; consequently your focus should be laser-like and your product should be uber-tuned. Then you have the inviting task of creating a brand and defining your own market. Don't scramble around begging for other people's leftovers: create your own rules and you exist in your own space.

THE WHOLE GAP-IN-THE-MARKET APPROACH IS AN OUTDATED FALLACY THAT SHOULD BE BURNT AND BANISHED FROM HISTORY.

With a narrow focus you can create a whole new category which can lead to spectacular long-term growth and engagement potential. And ultimately the opportunity to be the market leader.

'BrewDog have been fundamental to the development of the craft beer scene in the UK. It's not an exaggeration to say that BrewDog have changed the shape of British Beer.'
Pete Brown (beer-writing punk)

Back in 2007 craft beer did not exist in the UK and when it came to beer your options were industrial mass-produced lager or stuffy and fundamentally boring cask ale. We wanted to change that and instigate and build a craft-beer category in the UK. And we did.

Setting up BrewDog, we realized we would be on a kicking to nothing if we tried to take a share of the existing UK beer market. Slim margins and global brand domination meant there was no room at the table for the little guy, no matter how talented.

We wanted to create our own space and play the game on our own terms, not someone else's. We made our own rules and set about creating and establishing a craft-beer market in the UK. In doing so we controlled our price points, engaged a new breed and generation of customer, built a committed audience from scratch and created a whole new sector.

WE DID NOT LIKE OPTION A,
SO THE SOLUTION WAS TO CREATE OPTION B.

Since 2007 we have been committed to growing this new and rapidly emerging category that we created in the UK, and by default this strategy grew our business and ensured we became synonymous with craft beer and our passion for it. Niche is the new mainstream. To have any chance of success you have to start under the radar, on the fringes, out in the cold. What was impossible ten years ago is now a paradise of opportunity as boundaries, borders and distance have dissolved into insignificance. You need to create something completely specialist, something that initially gets a small amount of people very excited. Information can now flow freely and quickly all around the world, giving you instant access to your very own dedicated tribe. If, and it is a big if, what you are offering is worthy enough.

By baking your own pie you get to champion a category and become the leader and statesman of it. Winning businesses promote their category. Losers promote themselves.

NICHE IS THE NEW MAINSTREAM.

DON'T WASTE YOUR TIME ON BULLSHIT BUSINESS PLANS

Planning is merely glorified guesswork. Long-term planning is a vain, self-indulgent fantasy. Don't waste your time.

Back in 2006 a friend of mine started working on his business plan. We hooked up a few months ago, and guess what? The number-crunching clown is still working on his plan. In that time we've built our business globally and now employ over 500 people, all without the tragedy that is a formal business plan.

You need a strong mission for your business, a savvy understanding of finance and the ability to react at lightning speed. You don't need a business plan. Tomorrow there will be two types of business: the quick and the dead. It is time to go fast or go home. If you can't move at warp speed, take the next starship back to the ranch.

We live in a fast world; our lives are lived at pace. Long-term planning can't and doesn't work for small businesses and start-ups. It's impossible to keep up with the sheer amount of variables coming into play – it's more about quick spontaneous thinking than referring to an outdated plan. So don't plan for tomorrow, kick some hard-core ass today. Shoot first and ask questions later. All whilst basking in the glowing realization that if you had planned everything to the last detail the speed of the compounding forces of change in today's world would have rendered your plan woefully redundant before you had time to implement it.

So become a speed junkie and hammer it. Embrace the changes and roll with it. Be fast, fearless and forthright. Act, don't plan. If you delay, you merely postpone receiving immensely valuable real-world feedback which you can use to inform future decisions and strategy. Let loose with brave, enterprising and uncompromising action and let the market and the customer hone and refine your future moves. Real-world realizations are invaluable. Learn from them and let your strategy be shaped by the decisions you make.

SO DON'T PLAN FOR TOMORROW, KICK SOME HARD-CORE ASS TODAY.

Let a compelling over-arching mission guide your decisions. Not a stupid plan you wrote in the past. Act first and assess later. Sometimes ignorance is bliss. The more you know, the more likely you will fall into the same traps which snare everyone else. When we launched BrewDog, we did not know how things were meant to be done, so we just did our own thing and found an untrodden path that was much more effective for us. If we had been more experienced, we would have just done the same crap as everyone else. Our naivety and enthusiasm gave us the impetus to truck on. And the learning curve was truly off the Richter scale. Operational flexibility will allow you to achieve your objectives. Just keep a firm handle on numbers and have faith in your mission. Your mission is your compass, it will help you stay on course through hell and high water.

Hold fast and keep the faith.

BEG, BORROW, BARTER, BOOTLEG

There is a very simple reason why so many start-up businesses fail – they spend too much of their hard-earned cash on all manner of things that they don't actually need. Creating a start-up means you need to learn to leverage all your funds and make your cash work ten times harder than any other more established business. Getting maximum bang for your buck, and embracing the punk bootlegger DIY mentality, will give you a fighting chance of surviving long enough to start making a difference. Become a cheapskate, a tight-fist and a penny-pinching git (not necessarily in that order). Do whatever it takes to save and preserve essential cash.

Cash is king so swear your unwavering allegiance. In any start-up your limited supply of capital is sacrosanct. It is the lifeblood and oxygen of your enterprise – literally. Without it, you and your business are dead in the water. You need to guard every penny as if your life depended on it. Because, in reality, it does.

During the start-up phase, challenging every single cost like the most cynical and narcissistic son of a bitch on the planet will stand you in good stead. In fact, having less is often a bonus. Constraints are just advantages in disguise and opportunities to be innovative and imaginative. Cherish constraints. Embrace them. They will sharpen you, make you lean and brutally instil the value of every single dime.

Don't outsource stuff like a hammerhead, and don't pay people with money you don't have. Not having the cash to pay folk is a blessing in disguise. External people don't care about your business as much as you do, and they sure as hell don't understand it like you do. So do stuff yourselves. Consultants, marketing agencies, recruitment firms are all just unnecessary garbage that poisons the spirit and the finances of any start-up.

In the formative years delegation is for losers. Even as you grow, be very wary of external agencies and partners. They all speak a good game and promise the earth but at the end of the day they have no reason to care as much as you do. In the early days of a business, caring an insane amount is what will get you through.

Thinking back, we did it all. In the early years of BrewDog Martin and I quickly became experts in barcode visualization, trademark registration, label design, building walls, building websites, accounting, invoicing, digging drains, grant applications, installing brewing equipment, video-editing, repairing bottle machines and loads more besides. We did not have any other option but to do everything ourselves.

You need to embrace the radical punk DIY ethic. The original punks were not content to be merely spectators or consumers so they built their own subculture, with their own skills, from the ground up. When punk music first exploded in the 1970s most of the best punk rock bands were recording, producing and distributing their works independently – outside the established music industry. Living the punk DIY ethic means not relying on existing systems, processes or advisers as this would foster dependence on the system.

When your aim is to smash the system, you need to be able to exist independently of it. By building your business with skills which you have or learn, you will be able to understand it inside out, and even more importantly stay in complete control of it as it grows.

You need to be an independent, an outsider, a nomad, a libertine. You need to be completely self-sufficient and not rely on anyone for anything. If a skill set is important to your business, then you better learn it and learn it fast.

So buckle up, buy a one-way ticket to Skinflint, and win on two fronts – save cash and know every aspect of your business like the back of your hand. If not, finish your journey at the Loserville terminus.

BECOME A CHEAPSKATE,

A TIGHT-FIST AND

A PENNY-PINCHING GIT

(NOT NECESSARILY IN THAT ORDER).

FORGET ABOUT SELLING*

If you hire a sales guy or gal in your start-up or spend too much time worrying about selling, then you might as well fire your own ass. And you'll sure as hell put a bullet in your fledgling company's head. Hiring a conventional sales person or focusing on conventional selling from the beginning is one of the surest ways to seal your company's fate in today's new business world.

Here are a few simple ways to avoid killing your start-up through over-selling:

Firstly, you need to make sure your product is awesome. In the early days of your business it's paramount you and your team spend time on getting your product offering or service right, not on hiring a sales or marketing person. Your product needs to be chopped, tuned and ready to roll. Made so awesome people are gagging for it, creating its own buzz and, in turn, fuelling its own demand. If it doesn't cut it and send people spiralling into a buying frenzy, then you'll need to work harder on your core offering.

In a shrinking world built on global connectivity, information flow and social-media overload you'd be amazed how your product will fast-track itself, if, and this is a pretty massive if, it is good enough. If you do something remarkable, all the right people will find out about it faster than you can imagine. And they will come to you.

So make your product awesome and the rest will follow. Making something phenomenal is the future. Twenty-first-century customers make informed choices and have wised up to the hard sell. Having sales people involved too early will mean you are pushing too hard with a

* Or at least for now.

product that is not right and your company will be destined to peddle mediocre goods and services just like everyone else. You need to create pull to be sustainable. And you don't create pull through sales.

This early fine-tuning of your product will stand you in fantastic long-term stead. Creating the buzz and hype through the brilliance of what you create is the first building block for your company's future. If you can't create something which is brilliant enough to sell itself, then you should not be starting a business. End of.

Secondly, you need to ensure that you and your co-founders are close to the action. Forget surveys, forget research, forget focus groups and forget feedback filtered through other people. Get off your ass and get in the game. Get close to your potential customers and draw your own insights. Live-test your product then learn and adapt. Pimp your own stuff and see what is actually happening first hand. Folk will love the fact they're talking to the person with the vision, and your passion will shine through. A welcome antidote to the diluted, convoluted noise of a marketing chimp.

As a captain, a founder, a leader, you absolutely have to be where the action is.

Thirdly, you need to realize that selling, as a concept, has completely changed.

Conventional models of selling should be consigned to a marketing museum, which would close down after six months, as the paying public have got better things to do with their hard-earned cash. The way you act, function and communicate as a business has a direct bearing on how you are perceived, and in turn on your sales. Everything you do is sales and all of your employees are selling all the time. Act accordingly.

At BrewDog we were almost three years old as a business before we first hired someone to look after our customers for us. Fast-forward to today and we have a small (and brilliant!) sales team whose main focus is liaising with our existing customer base and making sure we are working closely together with our key partners for maximum mutual benefit.

You need to focus on doing something truly remarkable, something great, something which people are desperate to get a hold of. Instead of pimping sales, we spent our early years concentrating on crafting world-class beers that people all over the planet clambered to get their paws on and we focused on building a strong company culture that would be the foundation of our future growth.

Rip up the sales manual. Conventional methods of selling are dying a slow and painful death. Passion, integrity and quality are not.

INSTEAD OF PIMPING SALES, WE SPENT OUR EARLY YEARS CONCENTRATING ON CRAFTING WORLD-CLASS BEERS.

GET PEOPLE TO HATE YOU

'Having enemies is a good thing. It proves that you stood up for something sometime in your life.'
Winston Churchill (world-saving punk)

You need to get incumbent companies, competitors, random people and, in our case, regulatory bodies to completely hate you. If you can't easily achieve this, then you can't be successful.

Never be about trying to keep everyone happy. Delight in polarizing opinion; all iconoclasts do. The Sex Pistols never set out to keep everyone happy, nor should you. Punk was never meant to be for everyone. Accept that you will make enemies as you gain fans and that this is vastly superior to being so bland that you exist in constant obscurity. Hard-core fans are better than average-joe customers. As long as you do something you absolutely love, as long as what you do is underpinned by an all-consuming and fanatical passion, then you need to be able to not give a damn what anyone thinks. Fie on those bland, indifferent philistines.

After BrewDog had been going for around two years, the media picked us up and reported our excellent growth and trading figures. As you can imagine, not everyone liked this. Particularly the more established brewers. By their own archaic yardsticks and decidedly average standards, they couldn't understand our meteoric rise.

Desperate men do desperate things; stupid men do stupid things. One bunch of desperately stupid Scottish brewers concocted a document that basically called us liars and cheats. It cited we had simply made our sales and growth figures up. To add fuel to the libel the chairman of Innis & Gunn (a Scottish beer company), Mr Sharp, made a statement, and I quote,

'It is a well-known fact that BrewDog falsify their accounts. They are widely seen as the laughing stock of the brewing industry. Like an anorak with nae knickers.'

I would personally like to thank Mr Sharp. I had his quote pinned up on my office wall for two years. I looked at it every morning, and it motivated me to redouble my efforts.

Pretty much all you need to do for people to hate you is to be successful doing something that you love. As soon as your little business starts to show signs of flourishing some peeps will love and support you, whilst others will vehemently despise you with every cell in their bodies. Your success will only serve to heighten the haters' sense of their own inadequacies. Trapped in a dead-end job, never having the balls to take a risk, the hater takes great delight and pitiful comfort in hating those who are having fun doing something they love.

There are many losers in this life whose sole purpose is to knock you. These line-toeing corporate swine don't want you to be successful. They are frightened and threatened by the new. Clinging desperately to the status quo to justify their lack of vision. They are human sheep, destined to walk, to talk and to sleep with the sheep. Dystopian shadow puppets on a mission to take everything down to their callously indifferent mediocre level.

This is good though. It is a sign you are on the right track. Haters have an important role to play, a higher purpose to serve: they help to define your mission and your brand to others. When your fans willingly leap to your defence, their bond with your company is strengthened, helping you build enduring connections with the people who matter most.

And when you manage to get the Holy Grail of other businesses copying you, whilst others are hating you, you know you have hit a home run.

So love your haters. For without these weasels you would not have built an army of love. This can be a little disconcerting at first, so bask in the realization that if you were not actually killing it, their misguided, naive and evil intentions would be directed elsewhere.

Not got any haters? Then you need to up your game and try a little harder.

PRETTY MUCH ALL YOU
NEED TO DO FOR PEOPLE
TO HATE YOU IS TO
BE SUCCESSFUL DOING
SOMETHING THAT YOU LOVE.

BE A PERPETUAL PUPPY

To slightly tweak and immortalize America's answer to Susan Boyle, *'Despite having the rocks, she still lives on the block.'* Although J-Lo no longer lives on the block, in the hood, in the ghetto, or any place close to a kebab shop, she does unwittingly make an astute business point. You can eventually be Goliath but you need to ensure that you never stop thinking like David. Still with me? You will be.

Small is beautiful but big pays the bills. A guy called Steve Jobs once said: *'Stay hungry, stay foolish'.* Apple have remained hungry and foolish as they have grown to be the biggest company in the world. But, here's the trick, they have maintained and fuelled their underdog, outsider, maverick persona. And over the years they have built an incredibly loyal and rock-solid fan base who don't know, and don't even want to know, what the hell a PC is. They are the perfect encapsulation of a think-small-be-big kind of business.

I hate traditional big companies. Companies full of stupid policies, companies where abstractions make decisions, companies where everything is governed by finance, companies where procedure dominates and where people come last. Companies where employees are forced to apply stupid rules like brain-dead zombies. Businesses don't need to lose what makes them great in order to grow. But sadly almost all of them do.

As soon as you start to build your business ignorant people are bound to ask what your exit strategy is. Exit plans are for gimps who weren't that committed in the first place. It sickens me to think we could build something stellar, that we passionately believe in, and then trash it for some fast bucks.

I also don't see what we do primarily as a business, I see it as a crusade: a mission to introduce as many people to our passion for great beer as we can. And I'm glad to say I'm in it for the long haul. Beer is my bastard love child and I could never give it up for adoption. If you love what you do, why would you? Folk who build to sell don't build for longevity, they just want the maximum for themselves, and they don't care what happens to the business. It's difficult to build a relevant business in this way, and impossible to build one like ours. Consumers can no longer be fleeced and fooled; they're smart cookies, and they see straight through the smoke and the mirrors.

The other deal with being a perpetual puppy in business is – you must never roll over. Continue to learn and to take risks as your business grows. The fast-track way to failure is to take no risks at all. Trying to play it safe in today's super-savvy inter-connected world is the biggest risk you'll take.

Think small, be bold, be brave and continue to gamble. A good risk invigorates the soul. Push your team with your vision and ideas. Scare them with your thoughts and, above all, scare yourself. Risks will focus you and sharpen your game. Just when you're feeling comfortable, take your next risk. Make sure it is the biggest risk you have ever taken. Then do it all over again. We like to scare the living daylights out of ourselves every six months or so. In the end it feels good to put everything on the line for something you believe in.

As you develop never lose sight of what made you grow in the first place. As you add people to the team, strive to not only maintain but actively enhance your company culture. Stick to your vision and mission like a dog with a bone. And as your team and business grows, stay true to your beliefs and culture. Having an ever increasing focus on your people and galvanizing everyone through continuing to take stupid balls-on-the-table risks will help ensure you stay awesome.

GET READY FOR STINGING
REJECTION, CONSTANT CRITICISM,
EXTREME FINANCIAL PRESSURE
AND TRUCK-LOADS OF HARD WORK.

KEEP THE FAITH, PUNK

'Some things have to be believed to be seen.'
Ralph Hodgson (poetry punk)

People in north-east Scotland hated our beers when we launched them. Completely hated them. They hated the flavour, the packaging, the branding, everything. We sold almost nothing at all for our first six months. But we did not care. We simply told people that we brewed the beers we brewed for our own enjoyment, not theirs. We were completely selfish and made the beers we wanted to drink.

We knew that if we stuck to our guns and did things the way we wanted to and never compromised that we would eventually find our audience and our audience would eventually find us. If we were going to fail, we were going to fail on our own terms and fail doing something we completely believed in. But we knew we were not going to fail. We believed. Always.

Some people may have found it hard to keep believing. Six months in and we were sleeping only a few hours a night, often on sacks of malt on the brewery floor. Martin and I had moved back in with our parents to save money. We were selling on average less than ten cases of beer per week when we needed to sell seventy to break even. Every day the bank's threats would become more severe as we constantly missed our loan repayments. We received a vicious torrent of eviction notices as we could never sell enough beer to afford to pay the rent. Never, even in those darkest moments, did the thought of BrewDog becoming anything other than a huge success even enter our minds. Our belief was steadfast and resolute. The difficult times just made us even more dogged and made us work even harder. And that was the only reason we survived that terrible first year.

The savage reality is that you are going to get so many knock-backs, receive so many kicks in the throat and so many setbacks during the early period of your business that most mere mortals would simply cave and throw in the towel. Get ready for stinging rejection, constant criticism, extreme financial pressure and truck-loads of hard work, where you are putting everything on the line yet it feels like you are moving slowly backwards. Obstacles, problems, challenges and threats will rain down on you from every possible direction. So be ready; forewarned is forearmed.

The fallout from your business dream can be devastating. That's when you need to dig deep and believe in your vision and mission more than ever. You'll need to have unrealistic levels of confidence in yourself and your team to get you all over the line. You need to square up to every problem without ever losing faith in where you are going and your ability to get there.

So step up to the plate and prepare for a serious workout. Face obstacles head on and think of them as opportunities in disguise. Find your own way and learn from the experience. Very often thinking around something gets you to a better solution.

You need to believe and you need to work hard. There are no short-cuts. No collecting £200 as you gleefully pass GO. No magic formulas. No real overnight success story that is not at least ten years in the making. If you want to achieve something, you should be under no illusions, you are going to have to work goddamn hard for it. It is all about belief, self-discipline and focus over a period of years and years. Nothing comes easy.

It is supposed to be difficult. If it was easy every mother would do it, rendering success worthless. It's hard, brutally hard at times, but the journey itself makes it worthwhile. It's a deadly roller coaster of a road trip but it's one that totally rocks.

BASED ON THIS CHAPTER,
I REALIZE I WOULD NOT
HAVE A CAREER AS A
'MOTIVATIONAL SPEAKER'.
NOT TOO SAD THOUGH.
THEY ARE ALL JUST WORTHLESS
MERCENARY SHAMANS ANYWAY.

WE SHOULD BURN THEM
LIKE WITCHES.

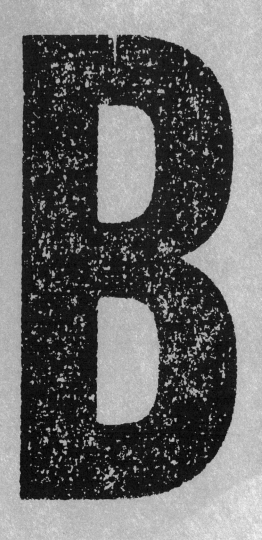

SECTION B:
FINANCES FOR VISIONARY RENEGADES

F inances. Those are for the number-crunching clowns with low morals and high salaries. Right? Wrong. Time to wake up, shape up and step up. Time to become a spreadsheet superstar.

Warren Buffett, an old business punk and the world's most successful ever businessman, said, *'Accounting is the language of business.'* And how do you know who is winning if you can't keep score?

Here goes, this is the single most important piece of advice in this book. Are you ready? Deep breath, find your happy place, get all spiritual on your own ass (not literally). You need to learn finance; you need to become fluent in it. You need to know accounting inside out, upside down and back to front.

There are no shortcuts, no fast tracks, no ways around. You need to put in the time to become an expert in small-business finance. It's that simple. You can't tear the system down from the inside, you can't find the beauty in destruction, you can't rule the raucous high seas unless you can keep your ship on an even keel. And, like it or not, your ship's keel is purely financial.

The business punk mindset is all about breaking rules. However, when it comes to finance, you need to be a Yoda-esque grand master of playing by the rules before you can even consider breaking them. Down the road, with experience and a stable cash flow under your belt, you can punk it up a little.

You need to be bold and walk a tightrope. If you are not stumbling, punch-drunk from one potential financial oblivion to the next, you are not pushing your limited resources hard enough. And you can only exist in this hyper-extended full-on risk orgy if you are in complete control financially and understand the commercial implications of every decision you make.

Cash flow, profit and loss are your new bedfellows. Buckle up and learn to speak finance.

WHEN IT COMES TO FINANCE, YOU NEED TO BE A YODA-ESQUE GRAND MASTER OF PLAYING BY THE RULES BEFORE YOU CAN EVEN CONSIDER BREAKING THEM.

THE BUSINESS PUNK'S FINANCIAL GLOSSARY

Being a punk does not mean not understanding your finances. The old-school punks learned the skills they needed to succeed and build their own culture. You need to take this DIY approach and learn the skills you need to survive and build your business.

The best way to terrify the establishment is to have the skills to beat them at their own game. You need to master the rules before you smash them to pieces.

Forgive me if some of these explanations sound like I'm a trainee accountant. But if you are going to change the world, you need to get up close and personal with these key terms.

ASSETS

The stuff your business owns. From cash to computers, from rolling stock to real estate. These are the things that get stripped quicker than a five-dollar hooker if you mess up.

BALANCE SHEET

A snapshot of your business. It will list all of your assets and liabilities to help you work out your net assets. The higher your net assets, the stronger the underlying business. The lower your net assets, the harder the fall.

BANK RECONCILIATION

Like all conciliations this is a real bitch. Unfortunately it's a necessary evil, a vitally important cross-check that ensures your accounts match the reality of your bank account. So when you say you're worth £5m you actually are.

BREAK-EVEN POINT

The exact point when what's coming in equals what's going out. The sooner you get to this point the better, otherwise it's open season on your ass. (This is nothing to do with *Point Break*, which is a shit film with Keanu Reeves.)

CASH

This is your liquid assets, all the money you can have, when you need it. Always remember cash is king, so treat it with respect.

CREDITOR

Anyone who you owe money to. Suppliers, landlords, bookmakers, the taxman and the Abba tribute act you booked for the Christmas party.

DEBTOR

A person or business that owes you money. Be all over your debtors like a cheap suit and try to secure payments at warp speed. Slow payers can screw your cash flow and ultimately you.

GROSS MARGIN

No, not that kind of gross. Gross margin is net sales less the cost of goods sold. The gross margin tells you the amount that your business earns from the sale of its products or services, before the deduction of any selling and administrative costs. *Capisce?*

GROSS PROFIT

If you were paying attention at the gross margin bit, this should be easy. Gross profit is the difference between sales and the direct cost of making the sales. No, this isn't all profit, so don't order the Hummer just yet. Or ever.

LIABILITY

A financial obligation or an amount owed to a company or individual. Also can be an ex-partner with an expensive lawyer or an out-of-control sales person.

NET PROFIT

Unfortunately not actually a net full of cash. Total gross profit minus all business expenses. This profit exists on paper. Once realized it is the stuff you can spend or reinvest. I recommend the latter.

OVERHEADS

What you have to pay out to run a business. All the fixed costs like rent, marketing, utilities and administrative costs. Begging, bootlegging, borrowing and bartering help to keep these costs down. Never get in over your head on overheads.

OVERTRADING

Another 'over' word, only this mother is a little more deadly. This happens when a business expands its operations too quickly, selling more stuff than its underlying resources can support – essentially running out of cash. *Ego vobis valedico.*

PROFIT

The crack cocaine of the business world. Pure unadulterated profit – the total revenue a business earns minus the total expenses. Enjoy.

PROFIT AND LOSS STATEMENT*

*(AKA an income statement, AKA P&L, AKA management accounts)

A financial statement listing sales and expenses and used to work out the gross and net profit of a business. Here's another statement – if you're in the loss bit, you need to up your game. And quickly.

REVENUE

(AKA turnover)

The amount earned before expenses, tax and other deductions are taken out. Keep that revenue stream flowing and row away from the rocks.

STOCK

This one is easy. The actual products or materials a business currently has on hand. Too much stock and you're screwed, too little and you're screwed. It's a high-wire act.

VARIABLE COST

A cost that changes depending on the number of goods produced or the demand for the product/service. This bad boy can go up or down like a yo-yo.

WORKING CAPITAL

The cash available to a business for day-to-day expenses. Remember, every pound/dollar you spend is another pound/dollar you need to earn, so work that capital hard, like your life depends on it – your business's life certainly does.

Digest, learn, apply and kick some ass.

THE BEST WAY
TO TERRIFY THE ESTABLISHMENT
IS TO HAVE THE SKILLS
TO BEAT THEM AT THEIR OWN GAME.

KNOW YOUR NUMBERS

Before Martin and I started BrewDog we did not have a clue about finance. I struggled to make sense of my own bank statement, never mind a balance sheet. Embracing the original punk DIY ethos of learning the skills we needed to be completely self-sufficient I went on numerous finance and accounting courses. I devoured finance books. I spent as much time as I could absorbing knowledge from the best finance experts I could find. I listened to podcasts and even stayed up at night watching online finance lectures.*

I went from finance twit to finance geek in record time, simply because I had to. In the last few years I have written for several newspapers on tax reform, advised the Scottish government on how they can positively impact the finances of small businesses and I have given numerous lectures on crowdfunding and our radical new approach to finance at universities and high-profile business events. I became an expert in finance simply because I had no other option. And you have no other option either.

Eighty per cent of all new businesses fail. And they always fail for financial reasons. The more you understand the numbers the less likely they are to crush you and your dreams.

Finances are the lifeblood of your business. They are the foundation of your enterprise's future. It's your job to lay them right. Get it wrong and you and your team are just busy fools, dancing to the tune of impending oblivion and destined to blame bad luck and circumstance for their own pathetic ineptitude. Build it right and success beckons.

---

* OK, I maybe only did the last bit once. But you get the point.

Build it any other way and some asshole in a pinstriped suit is going to come knocking and blow your house down. Venture-capitalist toads, faux 'angel' investors and greedy bankers pay their bills by preying on the financially unsavvy entrepreneur. They will swoop down and gobble you up like a vulture with roadkill, all whilst smiling at you with their red-wine-soaked teeth.

The first lesson in finance is cash flow. And it's a crucial one. It needs to flow. If it stops, you and your business spontaneously combust like the shark at the end of *Jaws* when Chief Brody blows him into smithereens. *Adios, amigo.* Game over.

Lack of cash flow can kill your business instantly, like being shot in the face with a sawn-off shotgun. Lack of gross margin will kill your business slowly, like being tortured by a bank manager. There are several other important factors to wrestle with and get a grip on, from pricing strategy and raising finance to overtrading and payment terms. For complete idiots I have included a simple glossary on pages 52–5.

Here are five basic financial skills you'll need to master before you should even think about starting your enterprise:

1/ **Putting together a cash-flow model**
2/ **Reading a P&L account and a balance sheet**
3/ **Cost of goods calculations and calculating gross and net margins**
4/ **Working out your burn rate**
5/ **Working out your break-even point**

You can't build a successful business without making some monumentally stellar decisions. And you can't make monumentally stellar decisions without properly evaluating your options. And – you guessed it – you can't properly evaluate your options without fully understanding the financial implications of those options.

EIGHTY PER CENT OF ALL
NEW BUSINESSES FAIL.
AND THEY ALWAYS FAIL FOR
FINANCIAL REASONS.
THE MORE YOU UNDERSTAND
THE NUMBERS THE LESS LIKELY
THEY ARE TO CRUSH YOU
AND YOUR DREAMS.

So time to crunch some numbers. Break out the books and break out a sweat. It's time for a serious financial workout.

Of course, as with anything in life, there are options. You could hire an expert. But then you're back to your cash flow – most start-ups definitely cannot afford to hire a great financial expert. Even if you can hire someone, you'll still need to understand finance to understand the expert and if you can't understand them then you will no longer be in control of your company or of your destiny. And if you are not in control, well, you might as well be back in your day job.

At BrewDog we spent half a decade learning the ropes of finance before we hired our awesome financial director. It turned out to be one of the best appointments we've ever made. And even sweeter because we all speak the same language.

You'd be amazed how many people naively start up a business and don't have a clue about finance. Those puppets should be, and will be, marginalized. They are doomed to fail. A financially strong venture, built on informed decisions, can weather pretty much any storm. And there will be storms aplenty once you set sail.

CASH IS MOTHERFUCKING KING

It's an easy mistake to make, but let's nail the confusion with both barrels – profit is not king. It isn't even prince regent. And cash is not profit. So let's get back to the title. Cash is most definitely the king. Profit is merely the fuel and not the destination. But cash, cash is the oxygen and the lifeblood.

There are indeed few certainties in life. But. Without:

1/ Cash

2/ Managing your cash like a demented cold war spy with OCD

I guarantee you that your business will fail, just like the vast majority of all businesses fail. All businesses that fail do so for financial reasons. And the financial reason they fail is always cash-flow-related.

Countless profitable businesses go bust every day because they run out of cash. It's hard to comprehend that successful, established, highly profitable businesses can implode into oblivion. But they do. And the reason is simple – profits exist on paper, cash exists in the real world. You can't pay staff, debtors, suppliers and rent with profits; you can only pay them with cash. Companies that can't pay their bills last about as long as dogs that chase cars. Sooner or later they're going to get smashed.

Cash is king and we need to ensure it stays in power and reigns sovereign. We need to bolster it. We need to religiously monitor cash flow and always look for innovative ways to boost it. Here, seemingly small details can make a massive difference. You will need to focus on:

1/ **Customer payment terms** – keep credit terms tight and enforce them with an iron fist. Better still, don't give credit terms in the first place.

2/ **Supplier payment terms** – agree the terms and try to stretch the payment plan to at least thirty days, but preferably sixty or ninety. And then always pay on time.

3/ **Get trade customers on to direct debit** – that puts you in control and they pay when you say.

4/ **Have flexible banking facilities** – an overdraft offers much more flexibility than a loan. Your ability to get an overdraft depends on your ability to seduce a banker.

5/ **Do daily bank reconciliations** – to ensure you stay on top of things. Not reconciling your bank account daily is like not checking if you are breathing.

6/ **Pre-load the account for bigger costs** – like monthly payroll and capital-expenditure projects. You will need to ensure you have the cash to fund your growth.

Cash flow is the main constraint to growth, and to really put a dent in the world you are going to have to grow exponentially and to do that you are going to push your cash flow to its limits and beyond. Unless you can understand your cash flow intimately, you can't take it into the danger zone.

We spent the first five years of BrewDog on an absolute knife-edge cash-wise. The margins for error were wafer thin as we pushed our inadequate resources to their absolute limits. We were often flying high but at the same time within a few pennies of disaster. And therein lies the crux. Growing a small company quickly is absolutely not for the faint of heart. In a small fast-growth ambitious company, unless you are constantly teetering on the edge of financial oblivion you are not stretching your limited supply of cash hard enough. Comfort zones are places where average people do mediocre things. If you are even the tiniest bit comfortable then you need to push harder.

Almost half of my time in the early days was spent furiously juggling payments, debits, credits, suppliers, customers, banks and payroll. I was always looking for an opportunity to cobble together enough extra cash to add additional equipment, people or premises to our business at the earliest opportunity to fuel our constant growth. And I was constantly looking for additional funding from any source imaginable. We always managed to pay all our staff, but for the first three years Martin and I very seldom managed to pay ourselves.

Like the very best racing driver, you need to live on the brink of risk and opportunity. You need to push yourself and your restricted resources to their absolute limit in a frenzy of adrenalin, jeopardy and nerve. You need all of your focus, skills and attention just to stay on the track, to stay in the game and keep your heart beating and to ensure you are pushing hard enough.

As you stare into the business abyss think about your king. Salute him, hail him, praise him and above all keep him flowing. Understand him, manage him, master him and you'll succeed.

But be in no doubt, without him you're right royally screwed.

PROFIT IS NOT KING.

IT ISN'T EVEN PRINCE REGENT.

THE PARADOX OF GROWTH: THE CASH-FLOW BLACK HOLE

This is the true paradox of growth. The faster you grow, the more cash you need just to continue treading water and keep your head above the waves. The more products you sell, the more cash you will need for stock and the larger your debtor book will be. Plus you will have to invest more in your team and infrastructure.

Look at the company's performance in the table on page 66. At first glance the stats look good, it's doubled growth and doubled profits. But the reality is that it's screwed. It's now in liquidation with a £1.5m gap in its finances. So what the hell happened?

This company has been sucked into a financial black hole. The sales growth and profit growth are brilliant. But to meet increased sales stock inevitably has to increase and this uplift in stockholding ties up £1m in working capital. With sales increasing, so have the debtors; often growing sales involves selling to bigger customers who always take longer to pay. The increase in stock and debtors smashes a £1.5m-sized crater in your cash flow. This model is pretty simple and does not take account of infrastructure and overheads, all of which would further hammer the cash flow in the example.

The company is definitely growing and solidly profitable, however its obituary is already written. You can't pay your wages and your bills with stock and with debtors. You can only pay them in cash. And if you can't pay your bills, then it is game over.

THIS SIMPLE EXAMPLE SHOWS HOW PROFITABLE
COMPANIES CAN SPONTANEOUSLY COMBUST.

	(2012)	(2013)	
SALES	£5M	£10M	GREAT SALES GROWTH. BRAVO.
STOCK	£1M	£2M	TO MEET THE SALES INCREASE YOUR STOCK HAS GONE UP.
DEBTORS	£1M	£2.5M	BECAUSE YOU HAVE SOLD MORE, MORE PEOPLE OWE YOU MONEY.
PROFIT	£0.5M	£1M	YOUR PROFIT HAS DOUBLED. BRAVO.
CASH	0	-£1.5M	BUT THE INEVITABLE INCREASE IN STOCK AND DEBTORS HAS JUST SIGNED YOUR DEATH WARRANT.

There are a staggering number of companies which get snatched away from their founder when their cash flow falters. The pinstriped vultures will swoop at just the slightest hint of adversity, raping and pillaging your dreams and your mission with their greed-ridden claws.

To avoid this fate, you need to have a robust financial strategy in place to fund the increased demands on your cash flow, as the last place you want to be is following these hammerheads into the same black hole. Even if there is a 573,000,000,000 to 1 probability of Stephen Hawking being in there.

The lifeblood of your business is cash. If you can't manage a cash flow, then you can't run a business.

IF YOU CAN'T PAY YOUR BILLS, THEN IT IS GAME OVER.

BUYING IS THE NEW SELLING

Your product needs to be able to sell itself, and you need to be able to sell your company and sell yourself. And the time when this is perhaps most important is when you are buying. Buying is the new selling and you are going to have to be a great salesperson to always ensure you get the best deal possible.

You have to make your cash, no matter how limited, work hard. When you've made it work hard, make it work harder. Being small, you need to think big about your cash. You need to set a target of getting ten times the bang for your bucks an average company would get. If you don't make your cash work ten times harder than your bigger, richer competitors, you won't close the gap. And let's not forget they have a multimillion-pound head start. Time to give your cash a serious workout.

Say, for example, one of our fat-cat friends decides to spend £20,000 on marketing their big company's product. We aim to get a far bigger impact by spending less than £2,000. They spend £50,000 on a new website, we aim to spend less than £5,000 and build a far better website. Completely crazy, I hear you say. Don't call the asylum just yet. Here's the deal – leverage. We leverage the hell out of everything to ensure the power of every penny we spend is maxed out.

In every single deal and every single purchase you make you have to leverage everything at your disposal. You need to put your imagination, willpower and inner thrift into overdrive. Sell the people who are selling to you on your company's growth potential, on the brand association, on your ability to pay quickly, on your desire for a long-term partnership as you make them hungry for the deal. Spread the love. Your core offering costs you less than cash so you can always use that to sweeten a deal. A few cases of beer sent to our supplier's office usually saves us between 2% and 4% on a purchase – if we do that over a year it saves us millions.

Play suppliers and quotes off against each other, and make up alternative quotes if you don't have them to hand. Never be scared to make an offer which is too low when you are buying something and always be prepared to walk away from a deal which does not feel right or stack up commercially. Spend every last dime as if it actually was your last and ensure that your team spend every single cent as if it were their own. Just by spending your money a little bit smarter means you can make your limited budget go much, much further.

Spend small, think big. Leverage everything. Sell your mama if you have to.

MAKE BANKS YOUR BITCH

Pushing for fast growth means cash will be a scarce but vital commodity in your world. In any growing company profits are not going to be enough to cover running costs and overheads, such as staff, stock, premises, capital equipment, scaling up and, let's not forget, your debtors.

The challenge, and the trick, is funding all the above whilst still maintaining control of your business.

You need to collect some nuts (and by nuts I mean money). Become an alpha squirrel. Get other squirrels to march between your banners. Gather nuts all you can to fuel your ever expanding squirrel army. The success of your colony will depend on your ability to choose the best, biggest and most nutritional nuts whilst supplying them in abundance. And what better place to start your search for nuts than at the bank.

There are heaps of ponderous books outlining the pros and cons of various options when it comes to bank funding; sadly I can't recommend a single one. Better to assess the various options yourself – from overdraft to invoice discounting, long- or short-term loans and asset financing. If you don't understand this stuff, no corporate clown in a suit is going to help you, and you're pretty much ruined before the train has left the platform.

Here I'm going to focus on the schizophrenic dichotomy of dealing with a bank. At times you'll need to be indifferent, at others, a real suck-up. Enter the business bank manager. These guys want to buy the ticket. They want to take the ride. They want to be on the surfboard as the next wave hits. To be part of the next big thing. They're desperate for a trophy client to make them, and ultimately their bank, look good.

As soon as you've made it, banks will be all over you like love-struck groupies. The trick is to get them to show you the money whilst you're still in diapers.

So go for their weak spot and start a hard-core sales pitch. Tell them their competitors are ready to jump into bed with you. After all, we all want what we can't have. Sell them on your mission and on your growth potential. Schmooze them, wine them and dine them. Sell them a dream. Make them think you actually need their help, their experience and their guidance to fulfil your potential.

In short, get a suited, booted one-dimensional financial android to think in your terms and believe in you. Get them to fall in love with what securing your business might do for their career. They want to climb that greasy pole. If they think your business will help them do that, you will have them wrapped around your little finger.

So whatever you're selling, sell it here today and sell it hard. Convince them they need you and you need them. This is perhaps the last bastion of the archaic technique of 'sales' left in twenty-first-century business. Embrace it. Sell yourself to bankers, whilst retaining a healthy enough quota of cynicism so that you don't sell your soul.

In early 2008, when we were really struggling to stay afloat, we entered some beers into a Tesco beer competition. I went back to selling a few cases a week at farmers' markets and from the boot of my car and completely forgot all about the competition. I got a phone call a few weeks later informing me that we had finished first, second, third and fourth. I went down to Tesco HQ and sat there with my best poker face on as they told me how they wanted to roll our beers out nationwide and would order 2,000 cases per week. I did not mention anything at all about the fact we were just two guys (and one dog!) filling bottles by hand. Regardless, I accepted the listing and had four months to figure out how the hell we would supply them.

We put a plan together and went to our bank and asked for a loan of £100,000 for a small bottling line and £50,000 for additional tanks. At that time in early 2008 the global economy was in a tailspin and the bankers basically just laughed at me. We were not paying our existing small loan back and they said that there was no way that they, or any other bank, would lend money to us.

Undeterred, I then walked into the competing bank across the street. I told them about the great deal I had done with Tesco. I told them about how we were an awesome up-and-coming company. I told them how, despite our current tiny size, we would be an epic long-term partner for them. I told them that if we embarked on a business relationship we would cover it on our website and give them a shout-out on our social media and promote them to other small businesses. And, most importantly, I told them how our current bank had just offered us an amazing loan deal on the finance for our new bottling line and new fermentation tanks, but if they could match this deal we would shift all our banking to them. And they did.

By them matching a non-existent deal we were able to get the bottling line and tanks we needed. The first bottles rolled off three days before we were due to deliver them to Tesco and the rest is history.

The only business plan we had in year one was to make awesome hoppy beers and to tell white lies to banks whilst wearing cheap suits. You could argue that our strategy has not changed that much since then.

Res ipsa loquitur. Let the good times roll.

ALT FINANCE

BrewDog is an alternative small company, part owned by the people who love the beers that we make. They are our shareholders, our best customers, our friends, and the heart and soul of our business. Inspired by everything punk and on a mission to put the power back into the hands of the people we came up with a completely new business model.

Raising finance in a way that does not simultaneously sign your own death warrant is key to growing your business whilst staying in the driver's seat. Being a small alternative business means we have to think smarter and kick harder across every facet of our business, especially when it comes to finance.

By early 2009 we had pushed four lines of concurrent finance, with four different banks, as far as they would go. But we needed to go further. Of course the global financial meltdown didn't help our cause. But at BrewDog we like a challenge and we love a constraint, so it just made us innovate.

That innovation, Equity for Punks, which saw us sell equity stakes in our company online, was an all-out blitzkrieg. Fast, furious and ruthlessly effective, it was a game changer for us. We have now raised a monumental £15m in investment and created a legion of brand ambassadors all over the globe. In one swoop we added over 30,000 members to the extended BrewDog family whilst ensuring we had the capital we needed to build our new brewery and grow our business.

We revel in the fact that people as passionate about craft beer as we are now own a slice of our business. No greedy hustlers, no fat cats (or dogs), no investment bankers, no venture capitalists,

WE DON'T THINK OF OUR FELLOW EQUITY PUNKS AS INVESTORS. THEY ARE THE HEART AND SOUL OF OUR BUSINESS AND OUR RAISON D'ÊTRE.

no overbearing parent. Just loads of people who passionately love great beer.

We don't think of our fellow Equity Punks as investors. They are the heart and soul of our business and our raison d'être. They are the BrewDog community, presently 30,000 and counting, spreading the word of craft beer around the cosmos. They are our liquid legionnaires, marching between the banners of better business and better beer whilst living the dream with us.

Equity for Punks jackhammered the financial rule book and turned the traditional business model inside out. We're a kind of modern-day punk co-op that is ultimately about connectivity, culture and community.

So don't be afraid to come up with insane new concepts. Be inventive. There are rules to be broken, laws to be stretched, drinks to be drunk, and empires to be built.

CORROBORATION: EQUITY FOR PUNKS

BrewDog is underpinned and driven by Equity for Punks, a radical cutting-edge business model which we pioneered and developed. With Equity for Punks we sold equity stakes in our company via our website to people who enjoy our beers.

Since 2009 we have had Equity Punks I, Equity Punks II, Equity Punks III and Equity Punks IV, with four separate tranches of crowdfunding – each one bigger and more impactful than the previous. Between the four share offerings we have had over 30,000 people invest in our business, raised over £15m to help us fund our intensive expansion plans and shaped a completely new type of business model for small consumer-focused brands and businesses.

The first seven (yes seven!) legal companies we met to discuss the Equity for Punks project with dismissed it completely out of hand and told us what we wanted to do was impossible. Most people might have called it quits after the first three or four rejections, but not us – we were determined to execute our vision for a crowdfunded beer revolution. When the eighth company we met thought that what we wanted to do might just be possible, we gambled our entire future on making it work.

We went all out to launch Equity for Punks. We had one shot at making it work and if we were to crash and burn we at least wanted to go out with all guns blazing. We hired a 1940s tank, plastered it with BrewDog logos and parked it outside the Bank of England and the London Stock Exchange. We were on a mission to tear down the system. Equity for Punks was not about tinkering with the established order. We wanted to strap on the dynamite. This was more Guy Fawkes than Rockefeller.

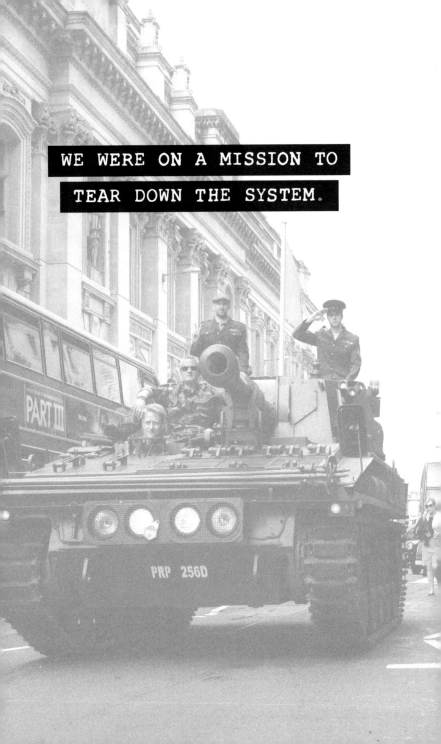

We wanted to drag small-business finance, kicking and screaming, into the twenty-first century. It was about empowering the change-makers, the misfits, the libertines, the community, the frustrated, the independents, the punks. Together we can, and will, change anything.

Our tank heist generated headline after headline as Equity for Punks blazed a trail through the UK media with an abundance of TV, radio, newspaper and magazine coverage, driving a huge surge of new investors. Our launch strategy was low cost but had a monumental impact.

With pretty much all other so-called crowdfunding platforms you don't own actual equity in the company. You are basically just pre-ordering some merchandise, some perks or some products, but not actually investing and holding a stake in the company itself. With Equity for Punks we wanted people to own part of BrewDog, to own a tangible piece of our company and our brewery and our website when we launched online in 2009.

We also thought that existing crowdfunding platforms had little credibility and offered potential funders very little security and we were concerned that they were not subject to any regulation. We went through a full and formal regulation and approval process with our share offering, going through the same standards as any large-scale public listing, giving our investors a level of security that you simply do not have with other crowdfunding platforms.

Our minimum investment in Equity for Punks was £95 and there was no limit on the maximum which could be invested. When we launched Equity Punks IV we smashed all kinds of records and raised over £5m of investment in the first two weeks of the offer, generating a further wave of headlines in the process.

As well as owning part of our company and sharing in our future growth, we put together a great package of benefits for our Equity for Punks investors, including:

- A lifetime discount of 20% on our online shop
- A lifetime discount of 10% in all our BrewDog bars
- An annual invite to our legendary AGM
- An annual invite to our Equity for Punks open BrewDay
- Exclusive first offer to purchase all new and limited-edition Brew-Dog beers
- £10 of BrewDog vouchers to toast your investment with
- A birthday beer, every year, on us
- A personalized Equity for Punks card
- Access to our awesome www.equitypunks.com site where you get to have your say in how BrewDog is run
- A twelve-month membership to our beer club if over £950 invested

In less than five years our investors have seen their shares in BrewDog increase by over 500%, giving them an outstanding financial return on their investment as well as a host of great benefits too.

In 2014 we launched our online share-trading platform, another first, as we become the first non-listed UK company to allow their shares to be publicly traded online. The online share-trading platform was a big success for us as we continued to redefine what is possible in terms of small-business finance.

From our perspective, the real beauty of the Equity for Punks model is not the financial side. It is in terms of how it entrenches the relationship between us and the people who enjoy the beers we make. We don't just have investors, we have a community of loyal and dedicated brand ambassadors, our very own army of craft-beer evangelists.

Our Equity for Punks investors are also our best customers and they are now interwoven into the fabric of our business. They are actively complicit in helping us grow and we all stand to grow together and benefit together too. We wanted to put an end to the traditional, slightly adversarial paradigm, with producer and customer both playing a zero-sum game. We wanted to flip the game from zero-sum to win-win. We wanted to completely align our goals and objectives with those of the people who buy our beers, to lock our customers in for the long haul and ensure we all shared the same objectives.

Our philosophy has always been to shorten the distance as much as possible between us and the people who enjoy our beers – and Equity for Punks is the ultimate incarnation of this philosophy. It ensures that we, and our best customers, are all exactly on the same page, and that is the key to what makes this such a radical and powerful business model. We all have an incentive to win big together, and have an absolute blast whilst doing so.

WE DON'T JUST HAVE INVESTORS, WE HAVE A COMMUNITY OF LOYAL AND DEDICATED BRAND AMBASSADORS, OUR VERY OWN ARMY OF CRAFT-BEER EVANGELISTS.

EXHAUST ALL FINANCIAL AVENUES. TWICE.

Look for money. Seek it out. Research all options of support for your business from the public sector like an obsessive deranged ex cyber-stalking the love of your life. Why spend your own money when you can spunk someone else's?

As well as the obvious places, there are several other ways to get more cash, legally of course.

Firstly, there are very often loans, soft loans, grants, job-creation assistance, tax relief and a myriad of other types of funding available from various public bodies, business development agencies, local authorities and government organizations. This type of funding is often very tough to get and intrinsically linked to job creation but given its potential to supercharge your growth it is definitely worth the effort. Over the years we have had to become experts in maximizing the amount of grant support we could get into our business. Indeed, BrewDog has only been able to grow at the speed we have due to the amazing support we have received in the form of grant funding. A couple of years after we started we received funding in the form of soft loans of grant support from Prince's Scottish Youth Business Trust, Support for Aberdeenshire Business, Scottish Enterprise, Scotland Development International, Regional Selective Assistance and Business Gateway. These types of organizations exist to help small and ambitious businesses grow, so make sure you know all about the relevant ones in your area and work with them as closely as you can.

Secondly, one bank is never ever enough. At one point we had four, which is kinda excessive. But, hey, who doesn't love excess? Don't put all your eggs in one basket. Have a balanced portfolio of funding; a blended structured finance package makes for a healthier, more stable business. Dealing with more than one bank gives you options, gives you bargaining power and gives you leverage to help put the right funding package in place to help your company step up to the plate and rocket into the big leagues. The banks hate it when you deal with more than just one of them, but playing hard to get just makes them even keener to put great deals in place for you in order to secure your business.

Thirdly, you need to look for ways to finance your business from within your business. Minimizing your stockholding will unlock cash which can fuel further expansion. Stock which is sitting is effectively locked up cash, and if your cash is locked up you can't use it to drive your business forward. Always look to lock up the smallest amount of cash possible in stock and extend payment terms to your suppliers for as long as you can. More effective stock management and negotiating longer payment terms with suppliers is basically free cash, and that free cash can be the difference between making it and the all too frequent small-business crash and burn.

Effectively managing your debtor book is a proven and tested way to bolster cash flow and increase the free funds within your business. It is a painful lesson that almost all businesses learn in their early days: there is a huge difference between making a sale and actually being paid for that sale. Be extremely wary of offering credit terms to anyone and also push for all transactions to be pro-forma (paid up front). Most companies learn this by being burnt and the same goes for BrewDog. Our biggest sale in our first year of trading was an order for £1,750 – we shipped it and we never ever got the payment. Our own naivety put us in that situation and the loss could, quite easily, have sunk our business. It was a lesson we only needed to learn once.

Bad debts and the painful gashes they leave aside, there is a huge difference between having customers pay you after 10 days and having your customers pay you after 90 or even 120 days. Having money owed to you by your customers is one of the main reasons there is often a huge disconnect between a company's profit position and a company's cash position. And it is this disconnect which suffocates so many businesses and brings about their painful demise.

Provided you get off the ground and have a product or service that people actually want to pay money for, the two main reasons you are likely to fail are tying up too much cash in stock and having too much money owed to you by your customers. Forewarned is forearmed so keep your friends close and your enemies closer and fall asleep each night with your debtor ledger and your stocktake on your bedside table alongside a loaded Luger. The two on paper are far more deadly and you need to be all over these key numbers on an hourly basis.

Fourthly, an often underutilized form of business funding is looking for loans or other types of financing from your suppliers. Your suppliers are all keen to develop their businesses too and the easiest way for them to do that is to supply companies which are growing, enabling them to grow by default. Thus, as a quickly growing business, suppliers will be dead keen to do all they can to work with you. Lagunitas, a superb high-growth American craft brewery, built their business for years on the back of loans from their bottle supplier. As they grew, so did their bottle requirements, meaning the bottle business grew too. The bottle company charged a slightly higher rate of interest than the bank would have, ensuring a higher rate of return for them and also that they locked in a huge customer and sold loads of bottles. It was high risk on behalf of the supplier, but with Lagunitas now the third biggest craft brewer in America, the unorthodox strategy paid off for both brewer and bottle manufacturer.

Funding from suppliers needn't necessarily take the form of a formal loan. Just extending your payment terms with them, often in exchange for paying an extra per cent on an invoice, can significantly enhance your financial position.

Finally, lease to buy when it comes to buildings, premises, offices, factories and retail outlets is also a great option which many developers and builders will happily consider. This gives you the huge advantage of being able to have something custom built to your requirements and the even bigger advantage of not having to finance it up front.

Chase down every cent. Pimp every pound. A man needs funding, particularly when he has no money. You need to become an expert in completely exhausting every finance avenue you can imagine, and then exhaust all the ones that you can't imagine too. Or get better at imagining.

CHASE DOWN EVERY CENT.

PIMP EVERY POUND.

DEFEND YOUR GROSS MARGIN LIKE A JUNKYARD ROTTWEILER

Any two-bit door-to-door salesman can sell on price. Selling on price is business suicide. You may survive for a while, but it's just a matter of time before it screws you.

You need to decide on a price and stick to it with a steely steadfastness. You need to be unfaltering and unerring on this; every trade buyer is going to try to beat down your price. You need to stick resolutely to your guns. You determine what you do, you get to determine what you charge for it and it is up to the potential customer to decide if they want it or not. If you make something good, create a buzz and people want it, they'll be prepared to put their hands in their pockets to get it. Never try to influence this decision with price. It's an easy road to juice up turnover but don't take it. If you price down you down-sell everything, and there's no going back.

IF YOU PRICE DOWN YOU DOWN-SELL EVERYTHING, AND THERE'S NO GOING BACK.

Like it or not, price cutting is the crack cocaine of business. You're both the junkie and the dealer. Like any drug, the insanely addictive short-term high will momentarily camouflage the long-term effects of underselling your product. And you will all too quickly get hooked. Your price-cutting habit will rapidly spiral out of control. Cut costs, make it cheaper, cut costs, make it cheaper. You'll be trying to save money on production. Reducing the quality of your product, cutting corners, until you'll eventually be cutting your own business's throat. And then the slow truth of this self-induced vicious cycle dawns: you can't make it any cheaper. You've slashed it until you have no margin left. And you've dumbed down your mission to boot. Game over, dude, all because you became a discount hobo.

So you need to defend your price point like a junkyard Rottweiler. You'll have to be prepared to walk away from loads of potential deals if the finances don't stack up. No matter what the offer, no matter who offers it, if it doesn't add up, pack up and wait for the next wave. If customers aren't ready for your awesomeness, rest assured they soon will be. Ride out their bluff, and nine times out of ten they'll be back with the right offer.

Your patience and steadfastness here will be justified, and they act as a direct reflection of your belief in your product and your integrity as a brand. So don't be a loser, be a winner, and stick to your guns.

Competing on price is a hiding to nothing. Small business simply cannot compete with the economies of scale of the major players – and they should not even try. Discounting or selling on price is a terrible strategy. So spend your time creating innovative and engaging ways to tap in to your customers. And if you've got something good, it won't be long before legions of loyal fans fall in love with your products and services.

In the early days of BrewDog we walked away from several deals because potential customers were not willing to meet our price point. And guess what, many of them ended up coming back to us and worked with us to put deals in place. That meant we got a decent price and a solid margin, which in turn meant we could invest in our product, our team and our brand, and continue to build our business. Furthermore, they respect our integrity as they know we will always bluntly refuse to compromise on product quality and refuse to play silly games on price.

Bigger customers are notorious bullies when it comes to price negotiations. From day one we took a bullish stance. Our position was straightforward. I simply told them:

'These are the beers we make. This is the value we attach to them. If you want to buy them, then that is great, and this is the price. If you don't want to buy them then that is cool too. But the price is the price: we won't discount, we won't bend on price and we won't compromise on quality. If you don't want to buy our beers, we are pretty sure someone else will.'

It was a bold strategy, but it paid off. Punk IPA, our flagship beer, is the biggest selling craft beer in UK off-trade and yet has the most sustainable price point of any craft beer in its category and is the fastest growing craft beer in the sector to boot. Our customers won too with this strategy. Our position meant we could continue to invest heavily in making our beers awesome, giving them a better quality product which they could sell more of over the long term. You don't have to conform to expectations and pressures – you can play the game by your own rules.

You get to decide what you do. It is for others to decide if they want to buy it or not.

In taking a bold stance on price, it helps if you have a diverse portfolio of customers. We have worked hard to ensure diversity in our customer base at BrewDog and our largest customer accounts for just 7% of our total business. Therefore losing that customer would not have a massive impact on our company, meaning we can be bullish in our defence of our price point and walk away from any deal we do not like. However, many companies end up in the predicament where their biggest customer can be 30, 40, 50 or even 60%+ of their total business. In this position you completely lose all your negotiating power and holding your ground on price becomes a battle you simply cannot win. This scenario has been an all too common cause of death for far too many small businesses.

Without a solid, sustainable, defensible and entrenched gross margin you simply do not have the capital required to grow your business over the long term. You must have a solid gross margin to be able to invest in your business and invest in your growth. If your gross margin is not strong enough, you are on a slippery slope to oblivion.

GRAB A LADDER

In holding on to your optimal price point you may like a ladder to help you on your way. Price laddering is a very useful tool to have in your armoury. Everything is relative. You need to provide the relativity. But not in an Einstein kinda way. Laddering ensures your customers get a great choice, and those opting for your average price point get a sweet deal. If you are providing a quote for a service, giving different options can help create laddering and when putting together a price list, having different products at different price points can increase both sales and profit.

> **PRICE LADDERING IS A VERY USEFUL TOOL TO HAVE IN YOUR ARMOURY.**

On a basic level, it works pretty simply. For instance, the IPA is the beer we want to sell, and the beer the customer wants to buy. However, its price is going to look comparatively high or low depending on the prices of the other beers on the list. Making sure there are substantially more expensive beers than it on the price list we submit to the customer will make it look much more attractive by subconscious comparison.

THIS IS A POWERFUL TOOL WHICH NEEDS TO BE APPLIED
INTELLIGENTLY AND INTERWOVEN INTO AN OVERALL STRATEGY,
BUT THIS VERY CRUDE EXAMPLE ILLUSTRATES THE PRINCIPLE:

PRICE LIST

(A)

LAGER
£20

IPA
£24

STOUT
£22

PORTER
£24

PRICE LIST

(B)

STOUT
£28

PORTER
£26

IPA
£24

LAGER
£24

HAVING MORE EXPENSIVE OPTIONS AVAILABLE YOU GIVE THE CUSTOMER A CHANCE TO TRADE UP IF THEY WANT TO, AUTOMATICALLY BOOSTING REVENUE.

Despite the fact that the IPA remains at £24, it looks better value on Price List B than it does on Price List A because of its relative price point compared to the other beers. The second benefit of price laddering is that by having more expensive options available you give the customer a chance to trade up if they want to, automatically boosting revenue.

You should never ever ever just offer one price when you are tendering, quoting or negotiating. If you are an illustrator quoting for a custom piece of artwork, don't just quote a price, quote a range of prices with a range of options and always put a crazy option in there. It will help you gauge your potential partner's price sensitivity. If you are a website developer, never give a potential client one price, provide a laddered quote with different options and tiers. This will help you boost sales and help ensure your mid-level options, which should be your sweet spot in terms of profitability, look great value. For example:

Magazine Cover Artwork Commission Quote:

Two-colour illustration **$1,200**

Full-colour illustration **$4,000**

Cover illustration plus ten screen-printed copies of the original artwork **$7,500**

Cover illustration with live stop-motion video to be used on the magazine's website **$12,000**

New Pet Shop Website Quote:

Six-page website **$1,950**

Ten-page fully responsive website **$2,500**

Responsive website including e-commerce portal **$5,000**

Responsive e-commerce website with user profiles and online community portal **$10,000**

Website built by actual pets **$1,000,000** – please pay in dog biscuits. Woof!*

Price laddering is a simple yet powerful business tool, so you need to embrace it and use it to your advantage. It will ensure you always derive the maximum possible revenue from a customer and it is also a great way to make expensive things look great value. You are missing a huge trick if you don't take the opportunity to always upsell and add value to every transaction.

Always look for opportunities to inject some humour and make people smile. Quotes and invoices seldom make people smile. You will really stand out if yours do!

LOSE MONEY, LOSE CONTROL

The ultimate goal for business punk finance is to grow your business as fast as you can without losing your business and without losing control. You need to ensure that you don't give the pinstriped vultures the chance to snatch your baby.

You should never ever ever lose money in order to grow. A first-class honours in Lunacy comes in handy for those who pursue this strategy. Of course you need to grow but you need to grow in a profitable way. Growing through loss-making is completely unsustainable and means you will eventually lose control of your company. So avoid being a loser by tight financial control, charging a realistic price for your product and leveraging everything you have to control what you spend.

Growth at the expense of profitability and growth at the expense of financial stability is not worth having. The old business saying that turnover is vanity and profit is sanity will be profound for eternity. Far too many companies just focus on top-line growth and boosting turnover without ensuring that they are driving turnover in a way that also bolsters the profitability of the business.

If your strategy is to grow whilst losing money, there are only two possible outcomes. You will either bankrupt your company or you will lose control of your company. Neither are attractive scenarios. You can't change the world if you are no longer at the helm.

Innocent Drinks started off as a great company: combining fantastic smoothies and admirable ethics they made a stand for everything good in the world. Innocent was a classic feel-good success story that grew from a market stall to a nationally distributed power brand. Then they embarked on the kamikaze strategy of growth by losing money and they lost control and lost their soul. As a consequence of losing money year on year, they are now owned by Coca-Cola – a company that is the exact opposite to everything they claimed to stand for. Their financial predicament meant they had no other option. The deal was the business equivalent of the Little Mermaid being adopted by Darth Vader.

If you grow by losing money, you will, sooner or later, lose everything.

YOU CAN'T CHANGE THE WORLD IF YOU ARE NO LONGER AT THE HELM.

LEARN TO LOVE CONSTRAINT.

BE AN OPPORTUNITY-COST WIZARD

Running a business is like having a non-stop conveyer belt of decisions racing in front of you. You will need to make a lot of decisions, and you will need to make them quickly and under pressure.

Your ability to grow a business quickly will, to a large extent, depend on your ability to understand the concept of opportunity cost. But the key thing is in taking this purely financial concept and applying it to non-financial decisions. Your resources are finite, you will not be dealing in ideals and you will need to get the absolute maximum out of every single thing at your disposal.

Your ability to allocate limited cash and limited resources will play a large part in determining your fate. And the best way to decide how to allocate your cash and resources is to fully comprehend the opportunity-cost implications of every possible decision you could make in any situation.

The purely economic theory of opportunity cost revolves around the fact that if you spend an amount of cash (say £50,000) on a thing (let's say a bottling line) then the consequence is not just that your bank account is £50,000 lighter but also that you can't use that £50,000 elsewhere. That is £50,000 you could not spend on opening a new restaurant, adding new staff or buying additional office space. So even though you spending the cash and having the bottle machine makes perfect sense, you need to determine if that cash can be better utilized elsewhere to help grow your business. In this example, the opportunity cost of buying the bottling machine was not being able to open a new bar, add new fermentation tanks or buy additional office space.

When it comes to high-growth start-ups, opportunity cost has further implications than purely the financial elements. Everything is finite in a small company. The more limited your resources, the more significant the opportunity-cost implications of any decision. Everything costs far more than just the price. Any decision means that you can no longer do a plethora of other things due to implications of the original decision on finances, space, resources, people, time and a whole host of other factors.

Just because you can do something does not mean that you should. In most cases, you actually shouldn't. In business, saying no far more often than you say yes is a prudent strategy.

Less is pretty much always more. The opportunity cost of a long menu is the doubt that arises in the customer's mind as to how fresh everything actually is. The opportunity cost of a forty-page website is that the reader gets fatigued, bored and misses the important points. The opportunity cost of having clothing rails jam-packed full in your shop is that the clothes no longer have space to be shown off properly. The opportunity cost of having 200 wines in your restaurant (apart from tying up loads of cash in stock!) is that your staff will be unlikely to know them all inside out and speak passionately and knowledgeably about them to the customer.

Space also has an opportunity cost. Put in loads of seating in your bar and the opportunity cost is that customers will be crammed and uncomfortable and not stay as long. An opportunity cost of a new bottling line in our brewery will mean we can no longer use that space for fermentation tanks.

Learn to love constraint and recognize that all resources are limited in a small company. Always consider the opportunity-cost implications on all of your resources, not just your cash, in deciding the most impactful course for you to sail.

Always try to maximize the impact of everything you do, back the big winners and don't waste precious resources.

RUNNING A BUSINESS IS LIKE
HAVING A NON-STOP CONVEYER
BELT OF DECISIONS RACING
IN FRONT OF YOU.
YOU WILL NEED TO MAKE
A LOT OF DECISIONS,
AND YOU WILL NEED TO MAKE THEM
QUICKLY AND UNDER PRESSURE.

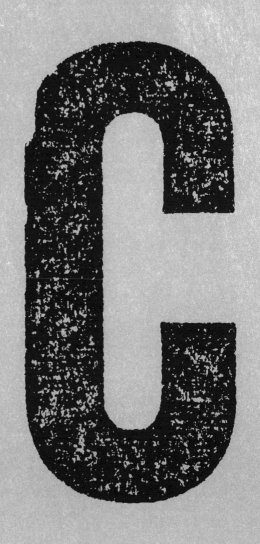

SECTION C:
MARKETING FOR POSTMODERN DYSTOPIAN PUPPETS

'What matters is this: being fearless of failure arms you to break the rules. In doing so, you may change the culture and just possibly, for a moment, change life itself.'
Malcolm McLaren (original punk)

When you are running a small business, you quickly need to figure out how to get some bang for your marketing budget, when you don't actually have a marketing budget. Our anarchic no-holds-barred post-punk marketing strategy has had the biggest single impact on our twin-turbo supercharged rise to fame. Full stop.

For the last few years we have had more airtime and more column inches than any other brewery in the UK as we rapidly raised awareness of what we do by dominating the beery headlines.

Not bad, considering our spend was next to nothing and we were up against some serious players, with multimillion-pound budgets. At BrewDog, when it came to marketing, we quickly learned how to punch above our weight. Putting some beer companies, weighing in at over 200 times our size, on the ropes in the process.

So how did we do it? By punking it up. By shaking up a stuffy industry. By taking a stand for what we believe in and by trying to smash to pieces what we don't believe in. By ensuring our customers could become fans and that our fans could become ambassadors. By taking on industry giants, and winning. And by storming the London Stock Exchange in a Soviet tank. All of this enabled us to have a phenomenal fast-track impact over the last seven years.

For today's businesses marketing is everything. Everything you and your business does is marketing. Modern brands don't belong to companies, they belong to the customer. And marketing dialogue is a two-way street, with customers actively engaged in shaping your brand. Gone are the days of the brand monoliths, who monopolized and dominated sectors and markets with old rules and outdated techniques. As they desperately cling to the ways of the past, you can be part of forging the future. A new dawn in marketing is here, and there are golden opportunities aplenty for those bold and imaginative enough to seize the day.

Don't stand still but do stand out. When it comes to marketing, playing it safe doesn't cut it any more. Safe is boring, safe gets lost, safe is over. Don't follow the herd. Lead from the front, break the rules, and to hell with convention and consequences.

Time to pimp your product, punk up your marketing and take the world by storm.

YOUR BRAND IS NOT YOURS

Your brand is your most valuable asset. If you engineer it correctly then it will be the most powerful weapon in your arsenal to change the world.

The most important realization in modern brand building is that you can influence your brand but you can never ever control it, nor can you ever own it. All brands are now owned and shaped by the consumer and you, as business owner, are merely along for the ride. As soon as you realize this you can try to influence the destination of the ride, but you are never truly in control. Managing a brand today is like being in the passenger seat of a rally car with the world at large behind the steering wheel in a headstrong mood.

A brand is no longer just a mark or logo. It is every facet of your entire business. It is an emotional reaction that exists inside the heads of people which you cannot control. It is all about perception. Not your own perception, but the perception of others. It doesn't matter one iota what you think your brand is; it only matters what your customers or potential customers think it is.

Your brand is the collated gut instinct of the world at large towards your company and everything you do.

This means that you, and everyone in your business, need to live your brand. You have to live the values and the mission, internally and externally, and then let the customer decide what your brand is about. Only by being consistent, engaging, open, honest and congruent can you start to build a brand in the twenty-first century.

Anything that you do, anywhere in your business, which is not completely aligned with your mission and your values is like a tiny little suicide. It is not death by a million tiny cuts any more; death can come from as few as ten inconsistencies or indiscretions. Little things can damage you exponentially. Mistakes are magnified and stabbed back into your heart. Don't let tiny little brand suicides stab your business's soul.

It's vital that what you do ties back to your crusade – your mission must drive all that you do. Consistency is the key. It takes years, if not decades, to build a robust brand: something that will stand tall and stand the test of time.

Today the only way to build a brand is to live that brand. People want to feel like they are buying into something bigger than themselves. Your brand must give them that opportunity.

> ## YOUR BRAND WILL BE THE MOST POWERFUL WEAPON IN YOUR ARSENAL TO CHANGE THE WORLD.

EVERYTHING IS MARKETING

Marketing is the sum total of everything that you and your entire team say or do. Even how you say what you say is marketing. In the interconnected digital age, everything your business does is marketing. Absolutely everything communicates something about your business, and ultimately your brand, which in turn affects people's perception of it.

The walls came crashing down long ago, although only the smartest of companies are alive to this new reality. Internal culture has to sync with external perception. The days of disconnect are over. Audiences are sophisticated, savvy and quick to smell marketing bullshit. Brand truths must ring true, inside and out, for them to be authentic and relevant.

In simple terms, marketing strives to shape people's perception of your business for the good. It seeks to align mission, product and service and draw the customer closer. The marketing journey, and it is a journey when properly executed, turns the potential customer into an actual customer and the customer into a loyal fan.

Until we start selling to other galaxies, the main marketing driver is emotion. Humanoid decisions are not driven by hard fact or logic, no matter how compelling, but by emotion. And here the devil really is in the detail. Consumers can lock on to the smallest of details to reverse-rationalize emotionally motivated decisions. What we think seldom drives us, but what we feel almost always does. Since tiny things can make all the difference, you need to ensure all the tiny things are amazing. Don't miss any opportunities to connect, resonate and build that relationship.

Small things make big differences when it comes to emotions, so you basically need to ensure that even the smallest detail of everything you do is not only astonishingly brilliant, but that it ties back into your mission. And that everything you do portrays you and your business in the way you want to, and need to be portrayed. It's a tough gig. But as with most tough calls in life, it's worth it. And it presents an opportunity for you to innovate, excel and shine.

Modern consumers like to discover for themselves, rather than being force-fed brands. So when all your hard work, and subtle seed planting, pays off, it does so with dividends. When people find out something awesome, quirky, lovable or cool about your business, it sticks. And the nugget they discover is much more likely to resonate than a more conventional mass-marketing approach. The great news is it's a whole lot cheaper, and a whole lot realer to boot.

Because everything is marketing, that means that absolutely everything is also an opportunity to build an ever closer connection with your customers. You need to bake your mission and your brand's personality into everything you do for it to resonate and build connection and momentum.

At BrewDog we are intensely passionate and irreverent, with a nuance of humorous quirkiness combined with a punk rock edge. We strive to get these four brand ingredients baked into everything we do. And always try to find opportunities to make people smile. Humour is the best way to make anyone fall in love with a brand, or even a human.

LISTEN UP PUNK!

It's a tough life being a beer
mat. Squashed under a glass,
passed around like a gypsy.
Despite my killer looks,
my life expectancy is short.
I am a beautiful lie.

So if you're going to squash me,
soak me and kill me, at least
do me the goddamn dignity of
abusing me with an awesome
BrewDog beer?

I am a willing martyr in
the craft-beer revolution.

Now, get back to drinking
your beer, bitch.

Take this beer mat for instance. Normally beer mats are pretty boring, just a logo and perhaps an overly engineered brand strapline. But not our ones. We decided to transform the mundane and largely ignored humble beer mat into a marketing opportunity and to use it as a way to engage beer drinkers and showcase our ethos. Consequently it has been shared over half a million times on social media, providing loads of free awareness and spreading the hoppy love.

Even how you hold your internal management meetings is now marketing. For our 2015 planning session we went free diving in a fjord in the Arctic circle with killer whales. How we held our meeting was even published by three different newspapers, giving us free publicity and bolstering our reputation. So much for having management meetings in soulless conference centres.

With a bit of imagination you can even turn the dullest of documents, such as an invoice, into marketing and simultaneously increase your chances of getting paid on time. You could add the following footnote to your invoice:

Please pay this invoice on time. Otherwise I won't be able to feed my dog. I wish I was kidding. If you are not intending to pay on time, please send some dog biscuits to:

BrewDog
Balmacassie, Ellon
Scotland

In today's inter-connected digital world full of intensely savvy Gen Y consumers every single thing you do is marketing as it consciously or subconsciously shapes people's perceptions of your company and your brand. And precisely because you can't control your brand you need to take every single occasion you can to try to shape your brand in the mind of your prospective customers.

Everything or nothing. It's your call.

NO BUDGET. NO PROBLEM.

'This is what punk rock is all about – using the tools we learned in punk rock to make the world a better place.'
Steve Hart (journo punk)

When it comes to twenty-first-century marketing, not having a budget is definitely not a problem. In fact, it is a massive advantage masquerading as a thinly veiled constraint. Advertising is dead, long live new media. You would be better off blowtorching your hard-earned cash, than spending it on advertising. At least then you would still have your brand's integrity intact.

Mass media is old media. It is as ignorant as it is irrelevant. All of which plays directly into the hands of the eager business punk. The traditional, yet totally outmoded, conventional marketing streams are all about the dollar, all about how much cash you can throw at TV, radio and printed media. If you've got it, flaunt it and then flaunt it even harder. Like a cheap jester clinging to their heyday of a bygone era. Smaller businesses can't possibly compete in this realm, nor should they want to, or need to.

Time to tear up the rule book with meat cleavers. Time to change where and how the game is played. Shift the focus from mass to niche, from old media to new. Online you can not only compete but you can kick the ass of these bureaucratic risk-averse incumbents, who've had it their way for far too long.

People don't want to be carpet-bombed with lowest-common-denominator dumbed-down adverts. Advertising statements and promises ring as hollow as the brands which still cling to this type of media. Consumers now want to be stimulated and engaged by something relevant to them. They want something to believe in. And the really awesome thing is, you can give this to them, gratis.

People want genuine, they want quality, they want passionate, they want real and they want integrity. The cornerstone of any effective low-budget marketing strategy is plentiful online content that reinforces how your company lives your brand, your mission and your values.

Any business has the potential to generate great online business. If you were, for instance, a fishmonger who specialized in the freshest fish from sustainable sources there is limitless potential for great online content. This business should:

- Have an Instagram account with a photo uploaded daily taken at the fish market.
- Have a Twitter feed updated daily that highlights the items which are fresh that day.
- Have a YouTube channel with monthly videos shot on the various fishing boats which supply the fishmonger.
- Have a blog with fortnightly recipes for great seafood dishes.
- Have a website with a section which outlines the importance of seafood from sustainable sources.

This will start building a following online; this will start building a community for your company; this will start showcasing the integrity behind your brand; and, in turn, this will build your business.

The example above is pretty obvious stuff. And nothing that has not been written about in countless other pretty substandard business and marketing books. In fact, I kinda feel ashamed that I have even written this last section on account of its mundane straightforwardness. But, of course, with a punk business strategy there is always a twist.

If you are happy being a really solid business with a way better than average grasp of marketing, then a strategy similar to the one I have outlined above will work really well for you and will stand you in good stead. But if you really want to put a dent in the world, then you need to spike it and add some dynamite to your online strategy. The pivotal factor here is that without consistent engagement and community-building activity, without loads of regular online content showing how your business lives and breathes your brand, then any attempt to add explosives to your strategy is just going to come across as shallow and phoney, rendering it completely worthless. However, if you can combine the dependable, transparent brand-building content with the occasional high-risk firecracker, then the results can be off the Richter scale.

We have spiked our everyday online content strategy with some high-stakes risks ranging from shooting a vlog whilst naked in a -30°C blast freezer, packaging a 55% beer in roadkill squirrels, parachuting taxidermic cats from a helicopter over London, projecting ourselves 150 feet high on to the Houses of Parliament, parodying the Russian president and petitioning the government for an entire week with a dwarf. There is much more detail on the specifics of these high-risk strategies later in the book, but the key element is that they would not have worked, they would not have gone viral globally, they would not have gained any traction, had it not been for our solid streams of content which established our brand and underlined our credibility and integrity prior to and for extended periods between these firecrackers being unleashed.

The other important factor in making our low-budget, high-impact, high-risk activities work was how we shaped all the communications around them. All the information we released massively stressed the link between these high-profile moves and our core mission. For instance:

- We used a dwarf to petition the government to introduce smaller drinking measures so we could use smaller glassware in our bars which best showcased full-flavour beer.
- We packaged beer in roadkill to shock people into thinking about beer differently. We wanted to create something disturbing which would challenge conventions and ultimately get people to realize there is a brave new world of beer out there just waiting to be discovered.

For a stunt to really work then it needs to be intrinsically linked to your mission and you already need to have a really strong following and a credible brand.

There is so much content competing for attention. The bottom line is that unless you actually do something that is worth talking about, it does not matter how much of a budget you have, no one is going to talk about what you are doing.

It is an unapologetically high-risk policy. It is not for the faint of heart. However, a few high-octane bombs can massively enhance your brand and provide a captive audience and loads of traction for your authentic brand content.

Chug, rinse and repeat. Same again, Fred. Building a brand takes years and years of consistency.

YOU NEED TO THINK GLOBAL AS OPPOSED TO LOCAL.

GOING GLOBAL

The walls are down, the world is round and we can all cross-border think. In your quest for global domination you needn't be scared of borders. To all extents and purposes, they no longer exist.

You need to think global as opposed to local and think free as opposed to paid for. You can now potentially reach the whole world for less money than it costs to put an advert in the *Manchester Evening News.*

Strategy and positioning should be designed to be global. Don't tie yourself to a location or geography. In our second year of trading we sold more beer in Tokyo than we did in our home city of Aberdeen. The beauty of the information age is that you now have a global audience at your fingertips. All of our social-media streams have followers from all over the world. If your content is good enough, you can cause a viral tidal wave from your bedroom.

Your global strategy should tie trade marketing and consumer marketing together. To date we have opened up over fifty-five export markets (no, that's not a typo, yes fifty-five). And we've done that with no export experience and no budget. All you need is a great product and the only investment you make is time. We have a tried-and-tested zero-budget technique we have used time and time again to get a solid distributor and instant traction in new export markets on the back of localized free PR.

Before you think about cold-calling any distributors (by the way, every muppet goes down that cold-calling road, the road to nowhere), export your mission. Get local bloggers passionate about your product. We sent free samples of our high-octane masterpieces to key beer bloggers in export markets which we were targeting. They would then cover us and our beers, helping to build a grass-roots buzz which started to prime the market. We then got the best distributors calling us pleading to buy our beers. They were excited about our mission, and had heard the buzz we had created in their country. Equally importantly we had already built up the demand for them, creating a market for them to distribute into and creating the all important pull from within the market place. All without them lifting a finger, or spending much of anything.

Fast-track to today. We now employ a small sales team but not in the conventional sense. Their role is to leverage our existing relationships and be our customer's point of contact rather than cold-calling like pimps. Their main goal is to build mutually beneficial long-term relationships with our key partners. And over half our revenue is generated from international markets without any direct contact with a sales person or any selling. We just receive, process and ship orders. Simple.

IN YOUR QUEST FOR GLOBAL
DOMINATION YOU NEEDN'T
BE SCARED OF BORDERS.

FANS, NOT CUSTOMERS

Shortening the distance between us and those who enjoy our beers is our Holy Grail and the cornerstone of our approach. We've had a wholly open approach from the beginning. Letting our customers look behind the facade has endeared us to them. We know all too well that trust isn't given, it is earned, and that it is earned through openness, honesty, transparency and engagement.

By engaging and connecting with consumers, you can recruit them to your crusade. By properly laying the foundations, they become actively complicit in your mission, and in turn help you to succeed. You need to become expert in leveraging technology to build relationships – you can build them with anyone, anywhere, in real time. Customers want to buy into a business that they can believe in; they want to buy from a business that bleeds, loves and laughs in the same way they do and that stands for the same things to boot.

From day one we wanted to build a community around our brand and our mission. Whilst we focused on the latter, our advocates shaped our brand. And together we helped to make people as passionate about craft beer as we are. By engagement and collaboration, by listening not dictating, by building a community, we have won over legions of fans. Many of whom we are proud to call our friends.

Having a community means that dialogue is exactly that. Which means direct customer feedback, helping to shape your offer and improve your business. By giving your customers a voice, and more important-antly by listening to them, the bond with your fans goes from strength to strength. Modern brand building is a two-way street.

Of course crowdfunding has been massive for us. But crowdsourcing has been equally significant. It not only helps inform our business but allows us to tap in to raw talent as well. We have used our community to seek out new bar premises, to help us recruit new team members, to source new trade partners and even to design new beer labels.

Here are some ways we have turned customers into fans and shortened the distance between the people who love our beers and us:

1/ Interactive Blogging

We blog consistently and religiously. We blog about beer, about ingredients, about our future plans, about our team and about our brewery. We blog about the things which are most important to us: our beer and our people. Our blog lets everyone see that we are completely congruent and that we live our brand each and every single day.

2/ #MashTag

#MashTag was the first ever beer designed democratically on social media. A hundred per cent crowdsourced #MashTag was beer by the people, for the people. We let our followers decide on every element of the #MashTag beer from malt and hops to special ingredients and the name – and we even let them design the labels too. We basically put our fans in control of the brewery and the brewing process. #MashTag proved so successful we have run it annually since its inception in 2012.

3/ BrewDog's Prototype Challenge

Every year our customers play a key role in shaping our beer line-up. We annually release four prototype beers in December and then let our customers vote online as to which one they would like to see as part of our permanent line-up. Some of our bestselling beers, such as Jack Hammer, Cocoa Psycho, Five AM Red Ale and Vagabond, all owe their existence to our prototype challenge and the power of our community. Power to the people. And beer to the people too.

We are essentially designing beers for our customers, so it makes perfect sense to get them to decide what our line-up of beers should be.

4/ The Great BrewDog Bar Hunt

Who better to choose our next bar locations than the people who will actually frequent them? We offer a £2,000 cash incentive in our Great BrewDog Bar Hunt initiative for our fans to help us find new premises. So far this scheme has helped us find five amazing new bar premises across the UK.

BY ENGAGING AND CONNECTING WITH CONSUMERS, YOU CAN RECRUIT THEM TO YOUR CRUSADE.

5/ Equity for Punks

Our Equity for Punks initiative (see page 76) was much more about marketing than raising funds. Playing back into our mission and again shortening the distance between us and the people who love our beers. We now have 30,000 shareholders and each and every one is a brand ambassador for BrewDog. Each feels ownership, and each spreads the word of Craft. Perhaps the most effective marketing campaign with no budget, ever. Equity for Punks entrenched the BrewDog community and ethos. It was effective marketing precisely because it was not about marketing at all.

Communities can also be built at grass-roots level and are just as effective for small businesses as they are for larger businesses. In fact, the smaller you are, the easier it is to start building your community. For instance:

- My local beer shop builds a community by hosting a home-brew club every Thursday night.
- BeerSmith (an app for beer recipe development) builds a community by posting a weekly podcast online about all things brewing.
- Musa, a great local restaurant in Aberdeen, builds a community through posting entertaining videos online showing you how to make its most famous dishes at home.

Whatever type of business you are in you need to start building a community and start turning customers into fans. Without a community and without fans a brand or a business is destined to be all too short-lived. Even with a small tight-knit core of passionate fans you can change the world.

TO STAND OUT, TAKE RISKS

'The bottom line is that you need to be willing to take substantial risk – and face the possibility of real failure – in order to open yourself up for real success.'
Noah Kerner (dance music punk)

Grow some teeth and balls. You need to take risks. You need to do some crazy shit. Scare your team with your ideas, and sometimes scare the living daylights out of yourself too.

To get noticed you'll need to make some waves. And we've made a few giant tsunamis along the way. Just ensure that whatever you do plays back into the very fabric of your mission. The real skill is making sure your over-arching crusade and company's DNA is woven deep into the core of any controversy you may cause.

The biggest mistake you can make is actually caring what people think. To hell with opinions, conventions and consequences. It is all just a game.

Word of mouth is still the most effective, and cheapest, way to make some noise. Unless you do something worth talking about, nobody will be talking about you. Don't shy away from controversy. Don't give a damn about offending people. Be true to what you believe in and have courage in your convictions. Playing it safe is for losers.

Unless you are occasionally petrified you are not pushing hard enough. You need to get yourself and your team out of your comfort zones. Comfort zones only exist to perpetuate mediocrity and anonymity.

HERE ARE SOME OF THE BIGGEST RISKS WE EVER TOOK . . .

CORROBORATION: HELLO, MY NAME IS VLADIMIR

Hello, Vladimir, goodbye, détente. There are many ways to get noticed. Giving worthy causes a leg up is one of them. Some companies give to charity, some support their local communities, some set up foundations. As you'd expect, we love to help the underdog.

Making a beer that we marketed as 'Not for Gays' was certainly a risk. However, Hello, My Name is Vladimir was a reaction to the Kremlin's homophobic policies. It irreverently showed me depicting the former head of the KGB in a pop-art style, with pithy copy, and of course some categorically awesome beer. I was half naked on a horse. It poked fun at the establishment and the political elite. A perestroika for punks.

We even dispatched a case to Moscow. We're yet to hear whether the Russian president is still a craft virgin. Or whether he can add Brew-Dog to his impressive résumé. Or whether it is safe for me to travel to Russia, ever.

MAKING A BEER THAT WE
MARKETED AS 'NOT FOR GAYS'
WAS CERTAINLY A RISK.

THE END OF HISTORY:
A BASTARD LOVE CHILD OF
BEER, ART AND TAXIDERMY.

CORROBORATION: THE END OF HISTORY

When we developed a 55% beer, the strongest the world had ever seen, we wanted to make sure the world noticed. So we packaged the beer in roadkill. We set out to create something as beautiful as it was disturbing: a bastard love child of beer, art and taxidermy. Hundreds of aspiring stoats and squirrels were interviewed and shortlisted for this starring role in the evolution of beer. Our concept was a ground-breaking marriage of beer and art which would break taboos, disrupt conventions and tear up people's perceptions about beer.

We got noticed and, more importantly, craft beer got noticed. By doing something grandiloquently controversial we were able to contribute to, and help shape, the ensuing discussions and open up a debate as to what beer is and what it can be. Shock tactics to change the world.

The End of History was on broadcast news all over the world, in pretty much every major newspaper globally and to date over 100 million people have viewed this story online. Oh and one of our stuffed brothers is now residing in the Australian Museum of Old and New Art.

So take risks. Big, stupid, heart-stopping risks. The bigger the better. Pressure is fuel, and we're serious addicts. Pressure keeps you hungry. Hunger keeps you growing. Without pressure everyone just defaults to being a lazy loser. Without taking risks, without looking failure square in the eye, you'll never achieve big successes. Achieving anything genu-inely relevant is completely unattainable without taking some serious risks. You need to lose the safety net and face the fear of smashing into the cold hard floor. Have a terminal craziness to do crazy shit.

LEAD WITH THE CRUSADE, NOT THE PRODUCT

People want something to believe in, something they can relate to and the opportunity to be part of a change, of a revolution. You need to give them that opportunity. They want to hear about your mission. They are bored hearing about products. Companies and brands regularly die and disappear, yet the spirit behind any revolution worth its salt lives for ever. It is precisely that revolutionary spirit which an ambitious enterprise needs to capture.

People are tribal. They want to belong. Give them something to believe in and you may just have a revolution on your hands. Rally them to your crusade. It is fundamental that you have a powerful and compelling mission. A reason for people to believe in you. Otherwise they won't bother. Quite simply they've got better things to do.

Leading a crusade creates a context of higher purpose and meaning, and it places your business firmly in it. It also helps create, establish and promote a category, which is much more powerful, purposeful and compelling than simply pushing sales of a product. Have a mission, establish a category, fasten your seat belt and light the fuse.

At BrewDog we're now at a point where we're a reasonably sized fish in a pretty small pond in terms of the fledgling European craft-beer market. The trick here is not to grow the fish, but focus on growing the pond. Giving the fish freedom of movement and the space it needs to fulfil its true potential.

A complementary way to lead with your crusade is to break out some books, swot up on your subject, and share. Don't sell a product, sell information. Out-teach the competition first and foremost, then out-sell them by default. The better informed the customer, the more discerning their purchasing. Spoon-feed information, force-feed passion, and soon your fatted goose will be ready to gobble up all your awesome products and services. And it will glue them to the very fabric of your cause. Information is addictive, knowledge is power. Pretty soon they'll be back for more. Provided the core of your offering is world class.

Don't compete on pricing or advertising but instead compete on education, information and passion. The more informed and knowledgeable the customer, the better position they will be in to make an expert decision. People also really appreciate it when a business takes time to share meaningful knowledge with them, which ultimately makes them smarter and better. The era of dumbing things down and trying to deceive ignorant customers is long gone.

SPOON-FEED INFORMATION,

FORCE-FEED PASSION.

Out-teach, out-reach and by default out-sell those mothers. Here are some ways we look to share our beer knowledge:

- We offer specialist beer schools and tasting classes in all of our bars around the world.
- We share our beer recipes online. For all of our beers.
- We have #tweetthebrewer sessions where people can ask us anything about our beers or how we brew them.
- We constantly blog about the art and science of the craft-brewing process.
- We post videos online showing how our beers are made.
- We produce infographics about the brewing process and paint them on our walls.
- We offer Punk IPA home-brew kits for sale, enabling people to get hands on with the brewing process at home.
- We have more trained Cicerones (qualified beer sommeliers) than any other company in Europe.
- We evangelize the good beer gospel on our own TV show, *Brew-Dogs*, which also goes into detail on the brewing process.

We are on a crusade to change the world of beer. And we want our customers to change it with us. If you are on a crusade, it helps to have something to crusade against and we hate industrial beers with a vengeance. We feel that over the last fifty years global mega corporations have destroyed the very essence of beer as they have bastardized, commoditized and homogenized beer to the point that over 90% of the beer sold around the world is the same lowest-common-denominator garbage. But the tide is now changing, and we are determined to change it even more.

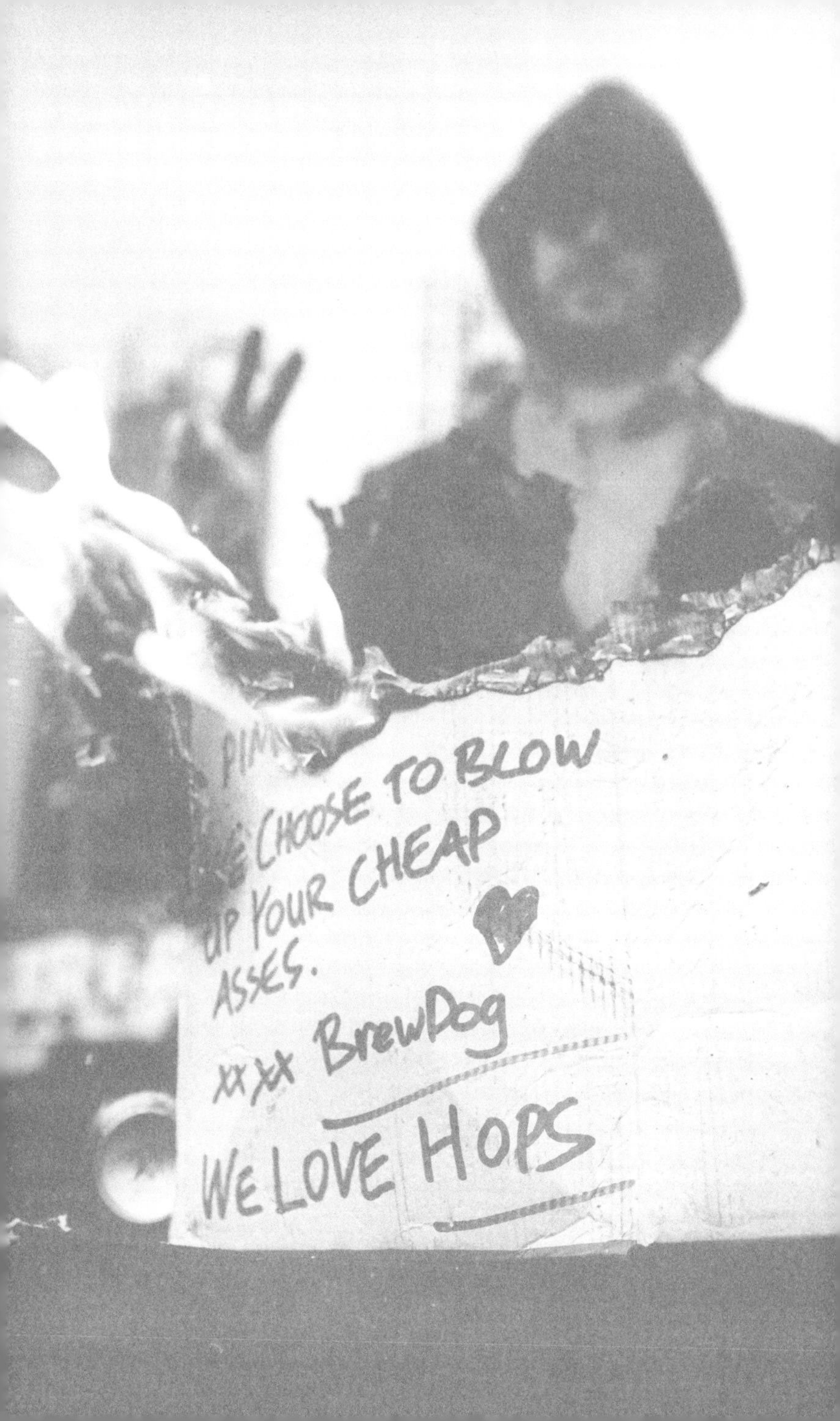
CHOOSE TO BLOW
UP YOUR CHEAP
ASSES.
xxxx BrewDog
WE LOVE HOPS

Our mission is to put the taste, flavour and craftsmanship back into people's beer glasses and open their eyes to a world of flavour and stylistic diversity they never knew existed. We hate bad beer so much that we are on a permanent campaign to destroy as much of it as we possibly can. And we also love filming this gleeful destruction. Our generic-beer-destruction videos have been viewed millions of times by people all over the world.

So far we have destroyed mass-market beers by:

- Smashing bottles of industrial beers with golf clubs.
- Blowing cans of generic insipid lager to pieces with sawn-off shotguns.
- Playing baseball with bottles of mass-market beer.
- Blowing bland beer to smithereens with massive fireworks.
- Playing ten-pin bowling with bottles of commodity beer as skittles.
- Putting TNT into kegs of generic beers and exploding them.

We have even held industrial beer amnesties where people can give up industrial beer in favour of craft beer. Underneath the fun there is a serious message and that message is our mission. Destroying industrial beer serves as a rallying cry for our cause and makes it easy for people to join us on our crusade to revolutionize the world of beer.

Whatever your business and whatever your industry, ensure that you out-teach the competition and put the emphasis on your mission and not your products. You need to have a huge focus on educating the consumer about your category and look to empower them to make the best choice possible. And they will thank you with their loyalty and custom.

MAKING NEGATIVES POSITIVE

Be smart, nimble and flexible. Recognize opportunities and create opportunities. Be a fully paid-up life-long member of the Opportunist Club. Jump on opportunities, nail them, give them both barrels. And ensure whatever you do, no matter how controversial or reactionary, sits with your mission. Being opportunistic is a great way to ensure exposure, bag some column inches and promote and entrench your mission, your brand and your brand values. It is also a great way to turn potential negatives into massive positives.

RECOGNIZE OPPORTUNITIES

AND CREATE OPPORTUNITIES.

Play an active part in debates and discussions and never miss a trick. Here is an example of primetime BrewDog opportunism:

CORROBORATION: FAKE BREWDOG CHINA

In late 2013 we were tipped off about a 'new BrewDog bar' in China. Now, this naturally struck us as quite bizarre considering we don't have a bar in China, and upon further inspection it would seem that we've made it big time because someone had actually opened a fake BrewDog bar! Our initial reaction was bemused, kinda happy, a bit flattered but simultaneously terrified. Here's an open letter we wrote and posted online to the emperor of this fine new establishment:

Dear (fake) BrewDog China manager/owner/emperor,

Thank you. It's not every day someone pays you the compliment of copying what you do. I mean, I'll admit we were surprised when we saw a picture of the bar you've constructed in our image in Changzhou, and maybe a little terrified, but mainly we were peculiarly proud. There's something that says 'you've made it' when a weird replica of your craft-beer brand is peddling beers through counterfeit taps somewhere in the world's biggest country.

I know that most organizations might reprimand you, condemn you and maybe even sue you for faking their logo and their bar concept, but speaking as the people normally being slapped on the wrists for rocking the apple cart in this industry, that would smack of hypocrisy. BrewDog exists to make everyone as passionate about beer as we are, and frankly your choice to build a fake BrewDog bar in Changzhou – rather than a fake McDonald's, a fake Starbucks or a fake Nike Town – suggests to me that we are getting there.

The fact that it is no longer the global mega brands alone that are being copied in China, but also the small craft-beer producers, proves to me that there is not just a slight change in the world's food and drink tastes, but a tectonic shift. Yes, your strange little bar exists on the fringes of legality, legitimacy and taste, but when the wheel spins it's on the edges that sparks fly – and we know all about that ourselves.

So – thank you, Mr Emperor. And good luck with your fake bar. I'll be along to visit soon – I'm looking forward to trying the Six Saint and the Funk IPA. I do still nurture a small hope though that imitation is the starting point of imagination for you. If next time, rather than knocking up a do-it-yourself BrewDog bar with an odd red logo, you go one step further and have a stab at your own craft beer, then you will really be on to something. You'll care more, and in turn you'll be better. You'll give more to the business, listen more to your customers and you'll make a metric ton of mistakes before you've even had breakfast, but most of all, Mr Emperor of Fake Shenanigans, you will have fun. It won't be about the money, it will be about the beer. And maybe one day someone will send you a low-resolution picture they found on the internet of a tiny bar somewhere on the other side of the world, with a makeshift version of your logo slapped on the front of it, and you'll feel exactly like we do. Like things will never be the same again.

Bye-bye,
(Real) James

What most companies would see as a PR disaster, we saw as an opportunity. There are always opportunities in the bleakest of adversities. Our refreshing and unexpected stance on this turned this into a major news story around the world. People loved our open, honest and irreverent stance on the fake BrewDog bar and this translated into a huge amount of goodwill and loads of new BrewDog customers and fans.

We now have loads of amazing BrewDog bars all over the world, but the fake one in China is probably my favourite.

FROM LO-FI VLOGS TO TINSEL TOWN

We've always worshipped at the temple of blogging. At BrewDog we blogged religiously from the beginning and we still do. Blogging will be your most important marketing tool, and the beauty is that it is completely free. In the arena where you have direct contact with the consumer, authenticity and integrity are currency and engagement is the anchor. Blogging is your big opportunity to really shine.

There are over 1,000 blogs and counting on the BrewDog site. We blog about beer, beer's ingredients, the brewing processes, our team, barrel-ageing beers and loads of other very beer-focused stuff. It's niche and it's geeky, but hell, we wouldn't have it any other way.

Back in the day, only a handful of people read our blogs. Fast-forward to today and over 500,000 hard-core fans peruse our digital output every month. We knew it wasn't going to be a walk in the park and we have worked hard to find the time to post great content online. And we knew we'd have to post consistently epic blogs to gain a loyal following. That's what we did, that's what we do, and it's paid off.

We were also early adopters of vlogging. Our first dozen Spielbergian epics were shot and edited by us. We just couldn't afford any outside help at the time. We shot them on the £150 second cousin of a Panavision camera, and yours truly was the editing monkey. I had to learn basic editing skills because we had no money to pay someone to edit them for us. From the start we had attitude and delivered an eclectic mix of information in an anarchic way.

One of our most acclaimed vlogs is 'Sunk Punk'. In this video we pushed the art and science of brewing to all new heights, or perhaps I should say all new depths. In 2010 we made history with the first ever beer to be brewed on the ocean floor. We wanted to push brewing to its absolute limits. The beer was not designed simply to raise eyebrows, it was designed to elevate the status of beer in the UK.

We also love filming destroying generic beers in creative ways. And we've had moments of digital education too. Our 'Instant Beer Expert' series of online videos gives viewers a quick overview of interesting beer facts and knowledge.

All our videos and blogs share a common theme – a passion for great beer. All delivered with our trademark humorous, irreverent and quirky BrewDog personality. And folk seem to like them. Some have had over a million views. The videos are cross-border, resonating with people all around the planet. The great thing about blogs and vlogs is they can be instantly shared globally. If you do something great, people can be watching it and speaking about it all over the world. Quickly.

GIVE IT AWAY

Sometimes astonishing things can happen when you give brilliant content away online for free. We were only able to embark on our remarkable Hollywood journey and film over thirty episodes of the *BrewDogs* show – about two best friends (Martin and me) brewing outrageous beers in crazy ways with the best breweries in America – because we gave away free video content on our website.

We knew people all round the world watched our home-made vlogs. But what we didn't know was that our videos were also being watched by the high-flying TV execs of Hollywood. After being whisked off to California to shoot a pilot episode and a healthy debate as to whether Scottish accents needed subtitles for a US audience, Martin and I ended up with our own hit TV show, *BrewDogs*.

However, there are countless other examples of free online content leading to huge opportunities.

Johanna Basford is an amazingly talented young Scottish artist and illustrator who BrewDog have collaborated with for some stunning hand-drawn beer labels. Johanna regularly shared her work, for free, in the form of a beautiful monthly downloadable black-and-white illustration. These could be used as desktop wallpaper, printed and framed and even printed and brought into technicolour through pens, pencils or paint. These downloads were shared all over the internet and loved by fans of Johanna's work. The buzz they created eventually caught the attention of some of the biggest art book publishers in Europe. Johanna secured herself a book deal and her first two books were worldwide smashes, with *The Secret Garden* and *The Enchanted Forest* having sold over five million copies, securing her a deal for four more books in the process.

We share everything with our community. As well as posting the exact recipes for our beers, we even sell kits so that our customers can re-create our beers at home. We share our future plans, our hopes and dreams, our successes and our shortcomings; we would far rather put too much information out there than too little. The future of business is sharing and great things can happen when you give up just the right amount of control. Remember, it is not even your brand anyway – it rightly belongs to the people.

SOMETIMES ASTONISHING THINGS CAN HAPPEN WHEN YOU GIVE BRILLIANT CONTENT AWAY ONLINE FOR FREE.

CORROBORATION: TV FOR PUNKS

BrewDogs, the TV show which span out of our lo-fi DIY vlogs, has became an international hit – it is now shown in over thirty countries around the world and we will soon start filming our fourth season of the show, making it the longest running beer TV show in history. The show has a cult following wherever it is shown and most importantly it gives us the platform to raise awareness of craft beer, educate people as to how beer is brewed and get them excited about amazing beer in general and specifically BrewDog beer. And all of this amazing global exposure does not cost us a penny. It truly is the next level of marketing.

Each episode of the show sees Martin and me rock up in a different city and hook up with a leading craft brewer there. We then set out to brew a beer in a way that has never been done before, be it on a train in San Diego or powered by music in Nashville. We also try to convert as many craft-beer virgins as we can as we do guerrilla-style craft-beer tastings in the most unexpected of places from old folks' homes to hair-weave salons and from submarines to shoe shops. We also love putting wild and unusual ingredients into our beers and we go on all types of crazy adventures, putting our necks on the line to find the most bizarre ingredients to use in the beers we are brewing. Each episode has a strong educational theme too, with 'Beer School' segments which outline parts of the brewing process and beer and food features where we work with top chefs and give people an insight into the amazing world of matching craft beers with food. It is all put together with our trademark mix of anarchy, irreverence, passion and quirkiness.

Each episode also includes a pretty outrageous brewing process as we look to make beer in ways that it has never been made before. In Delaware we brewed a beer at 100mph+ on the back of a pick-up truck whilst racing round a NASCAR track; in Michigan we brewed a beer twenty feet under the surface of a frozen lake; in Whistler we managed to brew a beer whilst zip-lining, snowmobiling and skiing down a mountain. We made the most expensive beer in the world in Las Vegas as a tribute to everything that is good, bad and grandiloquently ostentatious about the neon-lit metropolis that is Sin City. In Maui we brewed a beer using hot rocks from a volcano which were over 2,000°C and in Alaska we made a beer whilst marooned on a godforsaken island using parts of a crashed seaplane as our brewing system and ingredients that we foraged and found. In Baja we even brewed a beer Baja 1000 style, bouncing and skimming over the desert sand at over 70mph with 200 horse power kicking like a mule.

When we started shooting, editing and posting our own vlogs we just wanted to have some fun and share the passion we have for great craft beer with as many people as possible. Little did we know that a few months later we would be hosting our own international TV show. When we were finalizing the deal for the TV show, one of the things we were insistent on and pushed hard to ensure was that it was called *BrewDogs*. We wanted to guarantee that all the noise, hype and publicity fed directly back to BrewDog and really helped us to continue to build our brand. We wanted our TV show and brewery to be mutually reinforcing and both complement and legitimize each other. The impact on our business has been huge and we ensure everything we do in the show ties back into our over-arching mission of sharing our passion and having the most fun possible whilst doing it too.*

* Being on TV also means people say quite strange things to you. Whilst in Michigan a few weeks ago one person told me that I was not as fat in person as I was on TV and someone else told me that I have an unusual but symmetrical head. Both of which I took as compliments.

WHEN WE STARTED SHOOTING, EDITING AND POSTING OUR OWN VLOGS WE JUST WANTED TO HAVE SOME FUN AND SHARE THE PASSION WE HAVE FOR GREAT CRAFT BEER WITH AS MANY PEOPLE AS POSSIBLE.

DON'T BE COOL, BE YOURSELF

'Rather be dead than cool.'
Kurt Cobain (rock-star punk)

Be different. Be true. Be irreverent. Be selfish. Be ruthless. Be whatever you want to be, but forget about being cool.

Cool is subjective. Cool is, at best, a consequence. Cool is different strokes for different folks. Building your mission around cool is a kamikaze flight straight into the Pacific. It's a fast-track highway to nowhere. One man's cool is another man's carbuncle. Chasing someone else's perception of cool is one of the stupidest mistakes it is possible to make.

Do something that resonates with you and your team, and has the potential to resonate with your customers. Hold fast, and stay true to your vision. And don't give a damn what people think.

Forget all about target markets. To hell with this antiquated pompous notion that belittles people and perpetuates stereotypes. Only people pumped full of garbage on a marketing course have any regard for this most flimsy of notions. Having a target market and explicitly marketing to them is a sure-fire way to patronize and alienate pretty much all of the intelligent population. Anyway, people always want to be something they are not. Young people want to be old, old people want to be younger, sad people want to be happier and happy people want to be more challenged emotionally. So why waste your time trying to appeal to the aspirations of a made-up stereotype when you can just be authentic?

Don't look to others to realize your vision. Agencies and external creatives don't live and breathe your brand. You do. You've lived with it, day in day out. You know it, you care about it and you want to make it work more than they do. You know your customers better than they do. And you sure as hell are more passionate about it than they are. Joe Advertising does not have your brand ingrained in his blood – you do.

You have your brand DNA tattooed on your soul. Those soulless mercenaries just have dollar signs.

Success or failure, it's your call. Master your own destiny. Just don't chase cool.

> WHY WASTE YOUR TIME TRYING TO APPEAL TO THE ASPIRATIONS OF A MADE-UP STEREOTYPE WHEN YOU CAN JUST BE AUTHENTIC?

SECTION D:
SALES FOR POSTMODERN APOCALYPTIC PUNKS

There are only three very simple things you need to know about sales.

1 FOCUS ON THE PRODUCT

You need to create a product or service that is so compelling and brilliant your customers and potential customers actively seek it out. Don't push, create pull. Push is dead. Start creating some real pulling power.

2 BE OPEN AND HONEST

Build a customer base on trust. Create a mutually beneficial community, and make them feel part of it. Winning together is a much more compelling proposition than winning alone.

3 DON'T COMPETE ON PRICE

Undercutting the competition is a fast track to a real kicking. The only thing you'll end up cutting is your own business's throat. Stand firm on price and walk away from any two-bit hustlers.

So ends the shortest section in this book. Don't worry too much about sales. Sales are merely the by-product of being great elsewhere.

SECTION E:
BUILDING A TEAM FOR ASPIRING PIRATE CAPTAINS

F orged on the unforgiving North Atlantic, my approach to building and leading a team is also tried and tested at the coalface of one of Europe's fastest-growing enterprises. So listen up and take notes. There are no second chances. All self-respecting captains go down with their ships.

Perhaps the biggest single challenge you'll face on the good ship *Business* is the crew. Any business is only as good as the people who work for it. Period. You'll need to find, recruit, engage, train, develop, motivate and retain a bunch of totally amazing team members. That's a big list and it's an even bigger task. They'll need to be on the same page as you, passionate about your mission, and be prepared to graft on the high seas for as long as it takes, through hell and high water. It's a tough gig. But like all challenges you need to rise to it and take it head on. And in the end it's just another fantastic opportunity for you and your young bucks to shine.

Building a team in line with your culture is no trip to the mall. It will make your days long and keep you up at night. But (and it's a big hairy but) get it right, and it is time to break out those plans for global domination.

As with most things in your twenty-first-century business, when it comes to employees, the old rules are up for retirement.

They (the good ones) no longer want to keep their heads down and finish work at the same place they started fifty years earlier. Jobs for life are for the living dead. Might as well be a zombie. Today's best team members crave engagement, autonomy, development, challenge and reward. And guess what? If you don't give it to them some other mother sure as hell will.

If you can't get your staff to fall in love with your business, you haven't got a chance in hell of a customer to even consider liking it. Staff first, customers second may sound a little screwball, but, believe me, it is the only way to build for longevity.

Staff, like customers, want to belong. They want to believe in, and be part of, something bigger than themselves. You need to convince them that your crusade is exactly that, and to buy in with passion and purpose.

If you're going to kick ass and change the world, you're probably going to need a little help. Unless of course you're a president elect, Darth Vader or an opera-loving great white shark who has learned to speak and to play chess.

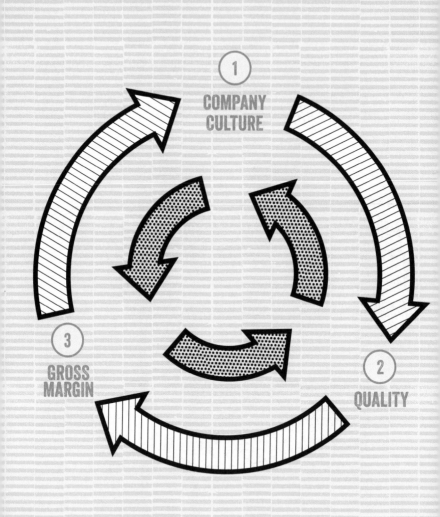

THE BUSINESS PUNK'S THREE PILLARS

A twenty-first-century punk business hell bent on kicking some ass has to be built on firm foundations. As you build from the ground up you will need to ensure that your concrete has three basic ingredients. Any great business today is built on these simple yet enduring and all encapsulating pillars. The three pillars are:

1/ Company culture

2/ The quality of your core offering

3/ Gross margin

Unless all three pillars are rock solid, you are destined to be a busy fool wasting your own time as well as everyone else's as your venture slides into oblivion. As the captain, it is your main focus to ensure these elements are all dialled in.

The most important thing about these three pillars is how each one depends solely on the other two for its own existence. Without the quality of your core product or service being exceptional you won't be able to charge a decent price. No solid price point equals a poor gross margin. Having a poor gross margin means you won't be able to invest in your team and build an awesome company culture. I'm sure you get the idea. It's a short circle but an unreservedly ruthless one.

Without a great team and strong company culture you don't have the quality of motivated, passionate people needed to deliver a great product or service to the remarkable level needed to justify your price point. No dollar equals no dream team. So break out the tin hat, stand back and cover your ears as the very fabric of your company culture implodes. Once you start heading down that track it's very difficult to put the Panzer into reverse.

Without a solid, sustainable, defensible and entrenched gross margin you simply do not have the capital required to grow your business over the long term. Namely, to invest in great equipment and in great people. Then the whole patchwork quilt of your dreams starts to unpick. And it does so at warp speed. Time to beam up another broken humanoid from the planet surface. Phasers on kill.

Monitor them, nurture them; they are your babies, your pet puppies, your pride and joy and the lifeblood of your organization. When times are tough, it is so easy not to ensure these pillars stand tall and true. But be careful; as soon as you let one of them wilt even a little bit you have also signed your business's death warrant. Get your three pillars firmly in place and you have a first-class ticket to ride.

Nail these bad boys and you really can go a few bouts with the world, and win. If you don't get the three pillars right, you'll hit the canvas in round one and be out for the count. The pillars are inter-connected and inter-dependent. Siamese triplets, joined at the soul. Each affecting the other. Get one wrong and they'll suffer together with everything crashing down like a tsunami of kamikaze dominoes.

COMPANY CULTURE IS 33.3% OF EVERYTHING

Company culture is a massively overused term. Very few people grasp what it actually means and even fewer comprehend its true power or understand how to harness it for maximum impact. Your company culture is the very fabric of your organization and it will drive and guide everything you do. One of your main tasks as a leader is to get it right.

A company's culture is a collective belief system and shared consciousness. It governs the ways a company's employees think, feel and act. It is your company's DNA, your genetic code and your moral compass. It is the internal incarnation of your brand and it must match the external image of your brand to be congruent and authentic.

A company's culture is what that company does when it thinks that no one is looking. The problem for a lot of companies with weak company culture is that today someone is always looking.

Studies show that employees working in a company with a strong company culture are more than twice as effective as employees working in a company with a weak culture. Just imagine how much impact you could have if your organization's team members were twice as effective as the competition's.

Your culture isn't a given and it has to be earned. You can't make it, invent it or spin it. It is actions, not words. And those actions can speak volumes. It is the by-product of consistent behaviour and it has to be real, grow organically from the inside out and it has to develop over time.

Artificial cultures are transparent. They lack substance and are thinly veiled; they are overly engineered smoke screens made of pure fluff. Faux statements, faux policies and faux promises all wrapped up in cringeworthy overly manufactured acronyms. You can't invent or impose a real company culture.

Effective cultures take time. They are built on clarity of purpose, consistency, pure passion and great people. You can start building a great culture by looking after your team and creating an environment in which they can flourish. And every time you are faced with a decision, you need to consider how the decision you make may affect that culture. Whilst you can't impose culture, you can cultivate it. It is organic, emergent and fragile. It is a huge challenge to nurture it whilst you are simultaneously pushing hard for growth.

Culture starts from you and your fellow founders. Ebbing from your passion, energy and shared values. It can be intangible and unspoken but it is always there. And how successful it is bears a direct correlation to the health of your venture.

Values need to be actioned. You need to live and breathe what you believe in with verve. The key thing is how things are actually lived in your business, not what you have written down. It is a self-fulfilling prophecy. You set the tone and create the culture from the top down and that culture becomes the reality.

A great company culture is the glue which ties everything together. It is the very fabric of your organization. It should drive everything you do. Maintaining and growing it is fundamental to your success. Your culture needs to be rooted in brand truth. It needs to be authentic, honest and real.

YOU SET THE TONE
AND CREATE THE CULTURE
FROM THE TOP DOWN AND THAT
CULTURE BECOMES THE REALITY.

THE BUILDING BLOCKS OF FOR EVER

Establishing a strong culture right from the off is crucial. Maintaining and enhancing it as you grow is the key to the culture locker room. Your company's culture is made up of a myriad of influences and a multiple of parts. Here are the five most significant and manageable ones – a sort of road map for the lords of culture.

1/ Kick-ass Clarity

You mission is even more important internally than it is externally. The most evocative and authentic external incarnation of a mission is achieved by shining a mirror at your company's soul. Furthermore, clarity of purpose and having a strong vision will be the glue which ties your people together. And the more together a team is the more effective they are. If your mission is singular and compelling then your team will be galvanized and empowered by it as they rally towards a common cause and a collective aim. The things that apply to your business externally are just as important, if not even more so, inside it.

At BrewDog our mission is completely clear. We exist to make other people as passionate about great craft beer as we are. We hire people who share this passion and our mission acts as a moral barometer for every decision we make as a business. We want to open people's eyes to a spectrum of flavour and stylistic diversity within beer they never knew existed and we ultimately want to make the world a better place through craft beer.

Folk want to be part of something meaningful. They crave to belong to something they can be proud of. And that something needs to be bigger than just a business, it needs to be a mission. They need to feel relevant and valued in helping bring about a whole new world order.

2/ Integrity is Currency

'One of the truest tests of integrity is its blunt refusal to be compromised.'
Chinua Achebe (literary punk)

Amen to that. Chinua makes a good point. A strong company culture is dependent on the integrity of the leaders in all parts of the business. You need to foster an environment of trust where team members have faith in the leadership and the leadership is accountable to the people they are leading. Remember, trust is earned, it is never ever given.

If hard graft is part of your culture mix (if it isn't, you might need to look for an alternative career), it will only resonate if it is lived by the people leading the organization. People mimic the behaviour and beliefs of their leaders so make sure that you, and the people leading your business, live and breathe the behaviour you want to perpetuate.

Integrity also has a massive bearing on your products or services. It is pretty hard to build an enduring company culture unless you are building, manufacturing, making or delivering something awesome, something which your team can really be proud of. People want to be proud of what they do and they want to make a difference. You need to ensure that the quality of your core competency gives them that opportunity.

At BrewDog we are committed to making the best-quality craft beers on the planet. This means that our team can take inspiration from, and pride in, what we are collectively doing. This directly translates into company-culture bonus points. If we, like 95% of the world's brewers, made lowest-common-denominator beer, full of chemicals and substitutes, it would be like pushing beer uphill getting staff to buy into it.

And it would be impossible to build a meaningful company culture. Game over.

3/ Join the Revolution

To commit mind, body and soul to something people need to feel like they are part of it. The way you make people feel part of something is through engagement. A company needs to have effective 360-degree communication and it needs to ensure team members are kept in the loop. You need to strive to create an environment where everyone feels like they are in the inner circle because they actually are in the inner circle.

It isn't enough for people to know what their business is doing. They have to know why it is doing it. They need to be fully armed with the reasons behind any decision. Only then will they ally themselves to the cause and work tirelessly to make those plans a reality. If not, they will feel alienated, confused and demotivated. And we don't want to go there – *Sayonara* and good night.

At BrewDog we always strive to ensure our team members are as engaged as possible. We have monthly full-team meetings for each team where we discuss our latest assault on humanity. We have a staff-only website called The Kennel and I send a weekly team email keeping everyone in the company fully up to speed with all things on planet BrewDog. Folk are far more productive if they know exactly what they are working towards, the progress the company is making, and how their role ties in to the big picture and helps make that collective vision a new reality.

To out-pace and out-smart an entire industry a lot of the strategies and moves you will take may, on the face of them, seem counter-intuitive. The most genuinely innovative concepts can often scare the shit out of yourself, never mind your team. Devoid of explanation they can look like the leadership has bought a one-way ticket to the land of the cuckoos.

Ensuring your team understand why something is being done means they are much more likely to put their heart and soul into making it happen. With everyone on board, there's no stopping you. Lock, load and roll into utopia.

4/ Power to the People

It is simple – your crew performs at their best when they feel they can develop and flourish. A commitment to learning, a commitment to training, a commitment to education and a commitment to promoting from within all equate to team members being more settled and more bought in for the long haul. If you strive to fulfil your team members' future hopes and dreams, they are much more likely to go the extra mile to help ensure the hopes and dreams of the company are fulfilled too.

At BrewDog we believe strongly in over-investing in our people. We believe steadfastly in personal and professional development. We believe resolutely in paying the best wages and providing the best benefits in our industry. We believe in constantly challenging ourselves to improve as an employer. And we know that without our amazing people we would be nothing.

WITH EVERYONE ON BOARD, THERE'S NO STOPPING YOU.

In October 2014 we took an unprecedented step and became a Living Wage Employer. For us this was essential to recognize how important our people are to our business and to a reciprocal future. We have a terminal addiction to making the best beers on the planet and to redefining people's expectations around customer service. All of this is only made possible by employing the best of the best (cue Maverick, Goose and Iceman, then sack the bastards for overacting. SFX: Welcome to the Danger Zone).

Companies need to wise up and max out. Smart companies realize, rather than minimizing wages, it is infinitely more productive and profitable in the long term to look to maximize engagement, loyalty, retention and productivity.

At BrewDog we offer loads of industry-renowned qualifications from Institute of Brewing & Distilling courses to Cicerone. We also run the BrewDog Academy (AKA the Harvard School of Beer – well almost). This is a series of free workshops led by senior team members and guest lecturers. We punk up a broad range of subjects, from finance to brewing science, social media, negotiating, beer tasting, logistics and packaging. In addition, we have management and leadership development programmes available to all our aspiring young bucks.

We're also big fans of pimping from within. This has always been a powerful motivator to our staff. But like all things in life it can have a downside; it's easy to get carried away and promote folk to levels beyond their current abilities and skill set. That's why we have a rigorous personal development structure. At BrewDog we strive to over-invest in the training and development of our people, ensuring they can grow their skill sets, competency, knowledge and confidence as the company grows. The vast majority of our senior management team have progressed from junior roles within our company. Having home-grown talent at the helm, who have progressed through the ranks, is a powerful building block of our company culture, which is only made possible by the personal development initiatives we have road-tested to destruction over the years.

5/ Culture Vultures

Each new employee brings with them to the group their own values and practices, meaning your company culture can change subtly over time. One of the most key decisions to make when hiring is assessing how good a culture fit a prospective employee is. No chalk and cheese here; like-minded, likeable individuals only.

Like the early bird, the early hires catch the worm. The first few people you take on will play a pivotal role in establishing and extending your company culture. Their importance in setting the tone for your organization cannot be overstated.

Looking back it is phenomenal how big an impact our first few hires had in establishing and anchoring our emerging company culture. Culture is pivotal at the early stage. However, all too often it gets neglected, especially with more seemingly pressing concerns like capital, customers and developing your product at the top of most agendas. Culture has to be a priority from the get-go and it has to start with the founders and then flow from the early employees.

Stewart Bowman, now our head brewer, has the dubious distinction of being the first human not named James or Martin to be employed by BrewDog. He embodies everything we believe in at BrewDog to an almost scary extent, exuding an infectious passion for beer, a great work ethic, open and friendly relationships, a punk edge and an encyclopaedic beer knowledge which is shared with evangelical aplomb. Stewart has not only been central to building our business but also integral to building and protecting our company culture and essentially making BrewDog what it is today.

Stewart, along with many of our other early hires, has been instrumental in shaping our company values. Martin and I directly interviewed each and every single one of the first 100 people we employed (this equated to well over 1,000 interviews), and although we were ridiculously busy during the first few years, this was perhaps the most valuable use of our time in the history of our company. It essentially ensured we hired people who would fit in with our ethos and our team whilst being ambassadors for our culture as we grew. We had to kiss a lot of toads before we found our superstars.

The torch of company culture is best carried and proliferated by those used to holding it and by those who have been with the business for an extended period of time. Those that it burns within. Those who have lived, breathed and pledged commitment to the crusade.

Get your company culture right and it's pure plutonium. Get it wrong and it's Chernobyl.

CULTURE HAS TO BE A PRIORITY FROM THE GET-GO AND IT HAS TO START WITH THE FOUNDERS AND THEN FLOW FROM THE EARLY EMPLOYEES.

INTERNAL = EXTERNAL

The zeitgeist of now means that all walls are down. From Berlin to Beijing there are no divides. There is no internal/external. Your staff are just as important, if not more important, than your customers. You need to live the same values on the inside as you do on the outside. We already explored this idea from the outside in, now it is time to look at it from the inside out.

Conventionally a company's culture is the other side of the coin from a company's brand. But in today's world the coin is spinning so fast that the heads and tails blur into one. Working on your company culture is actually a much more effective form of marketing than pretty much all traditional marketing mediums combined. Culture is marketing. Culture is brand. Culture now resonates much more with consumers than advertising does.

The only businesses that are worth a damn are those that pay as much attention to how things are perceived internally as they are externally. You need to live and breathe the external message and the mission internally. Mirrors are everywhere; you cannot escape them. Everything is reflected to the outside world. Absolutely everything.

Think of your business as a reversible jacket. Wear the inside or wear the outside, it is the same. Both sides do slightly different things, but it's the same jacket. Look after your staff and they will look after your customers and the people who are important for your business. It's that unconventional and that simple. Serve your teams and your people and then they will serve the customers with the same approach.

It will be impossible to get customers to love what you do if your team didn't love it first. First loves last for ever. Your team is your front of shop. They represent your business to the wider world. The more inspired, secure, engaged and valued they feel, the better ambassadors they will be and the better impression they will give everyone they deal with. You need to put in just as many hours making your team feel amazing as you do enhancing the customer experience.

The other consequence of ignoring any internal-external divide is that customers feel closer to your business if you give them not just a peek behind the curtain but the keys to the house. And it goes some way to shortening the distance between you and your customers which is the new Holy Grail of brand building.

If everyone is on the front line grafting towards something they clearly understand and passionately believe in, it's much easier for customers to understand why you are extraordinary. Your crusade must be seamless inside and out.

At BrewDog our mission is all-consuming. It's the reason we get up and the reason we don't go to bed. For us, it is everything. We are busting our guts on our insanely addictive crusade to make everyone as passionate about amazing craft beer as we are. And guess what? It's working. We are putting choice, quality and flavour into every glass. Elevating the status of beer. And changing the landscape of the brewing industry for ever, one bottle at a time. Long live the revolution.

Break down the walls. With jackhammers.

EVERYTHING IS REFLECTED TO THE OUTSIDE WORLD.

INTERVIEWS SUCK

Interviews and first dates suck. Awkward silences, pregnant pauses and excessive sweating. Saying anything that pops into your empty head, like, 'So, do you eat much soup?' or 'A friend of my cousin trained his pet gerbil to breakdance to Rachmaninov'. First dates become last dates and interviews are rapidly exited.

In fact, first dates are probably easier, thanks to the socially lubricating effect of alcohol. Maybe always offer your interviewee a drink too; we often do. A cold beer or bourbon on the rocks will help break the ice. You'll end up hiring employee of the month and avoid some psycho weasel entering your ranks. Do this for interviews and first dates. You can thank me later. Preferably with a beer.

Even if the interview goes well, interviews are a terrible way to find out if someone will be a good employee or not. The only thing you learn in an interview is how good that person is at doing interviews. And unless their job is to be interviewed, this is not really going to do you any good at all.

At BrewDog we try our best to do it differently. Not different for difference's sake but different to make a difference. Making candidates feel at ease and exploring their cultural fit.

In the formative years of BrewDog Martin and I did all of the interviewing. The first 100 people we hired were interviewed by a founder. It took up mountains of our time when we were too busy to sleep, but, in our view, deciding on the people who were going to join our business was the most valuable thing we could spend our time on. We tended to do a lot of the interviews off site and wrap them up in a social event. Bowling was good; they'd either strike it lucky or strike out.

You can gauge personality, test mettle and experience their cultural fit with a little social intercourse. How they handle failure or success in the lanes. How they interact with others in the team. You can tell a lot about a person by how they celebrate a strike.

If you're not sure the candidate is dynamite or a sideshow freak in disguise, take them for a test drive. Try before you buy. I don't mean ask them to resign, hire them then fire them (although we'll talk about the latter in a moment). Set them a small project, ask them to come in over a weekend or do some evening work. It's a great way to see how they perform and how they fit in and how you work together. You may not like them, they may not like you; it's a two-way street.

To sum up, we have two simple rules for hiring:

1/ They have to be as passionate about our mission as we are.
2/ They have to be the right cultural fit.

This way you strengthen your team, in turn your culture, and ultimately your business. We only want to hire people who believe what we believe.

Don't get me wrong, it's still a tough gig. Get it right and your business will flourish. Keep getting it wrong and you won't have a business. Don't sweat it too much though; when hiring, a 60–70% strike rate is good enough to make you a superstar.

You should always be in recruitment mode. Don't just wait for people to apply, you need to identify, approach and poach the people you want in your business. Friends, family members, random strangers, online cyber-stalkers and business acquaintances: you need to view everyone as a possible team member. I once approached and hired someone because I loved their Twitter feed.

Even when all of the above is in place, there will be occasions when you get it badly wrong. Sometimes an ass-kissing halfwit slips through the perimeter fence. You'll need to move quickly, in cold blood and with Panzer-like efficiency. A bad egg can quickly grow legs, feathers and a beak. Firing is harder than hiring but it sure as hell is quicker.

You need to do it for your own sanity but more importantly for your team. An underperformer or a poor fit culturally can quickly affect morale. Sometimes you just need to go with your instinct. I've had to let people go after a few days and I once even fired someone on their first day. They just didn't cut it. It sounds brutal, and it probably is, but it is infinitely better than the slow erosion of the company culture that you and your awesome team worked so hard to build.

DON'T JUST WAIT FOR PEOPLE TO APPLY, YOU NEED TO IDENTIFY, APPROACH AND POACH THE PEOPLE YOU WANT IN YOUR BUSINESS.

LOVE AT FIRST SIGHT

On-boarding is the mechanism through which new team members are inducted into a business. It is the start of a love affair of epic proportions. A love affair between your business and your new employee. The romance of a lifetime. You need to ensure that this affair gets off to the best possible start and that it is constantly lubricated, fuelled and consummated.

The first few days, even the first few heartbeats, of a new employee's time in your environment will be crucial. As you breathe life into their aspirations, they, in turn, breathe it into your vision. So the more inspiring and engaging your on-boarding procedure, the better that individual's performance over the short, medium and long term will be.

Great on-boarding will reduce staff turnover, increase productivity and boost company culture. Fact.

Their first port of call will be your new employee materials. A company welcome pack should do exactly that. In most businesses it does the exact opposite. At worst it doesn't exist, and at best it is full of turgid legal baloney. A more apt title would often be: 'Welcome to corporate hell, asshole, and you actually signed up for this dystopia.'

Make sure you're the author, and make sure it's written in your tone and it reflects your vision. Present your company through the eyes of some low-life money-sucking lawyer, and it's time to load the howitzer and kiss your, and your new recruit's, ass goodbye.

A staff handbook should be a road map. Something that gets you and your new employees the fastest way from A to Bigger Business. It needs to be as awesome as your website and customer-facing literature. It should clearly and succinctly represent your vision, values, mission and culture. Something you'd be proud to take home to meet your mum. 'Mum, this is staff handbook. Staff handbook, Mum. I am actually in love.'

Remember the walls are down; there is no internal-external split. Your brand is one. You need to hammer this mother home. Your customer brand and your employee brand are one and the same – two sides of the same coin. Toss it, and heads or tails it's the same result. Staff handbooks are just as important as customer newsletters.

As you grow, you may departmentalize functions and people. But don't compartmentalize your staff. Make sure your rookies feel part of the wider team and the bigger picture from the off. This helps them to see the scale of your operations and ambitions, in turn promoting synergy, camaraderie and solid links between all your shipmates.

YOUR BRAND IS ONE.

YOU NEED TO HAMMER

THIS MOTHER HOME.

LOYALTY IS
THE NEW ROYALTY

The best thing you can learn from a pooch is loyalty. However good or bad the day, my hound is going to stick by my side. Man's best friend is business's best friend too.

Sadly loyalty in business can be fickle. When you're flying high it's dead easy to shine. When you crash and burn it's 100 times harder. You only really find out what someone is like when things get tough, when people are under pressure and when the shit hits the fan. In extreme adversity you discover who has it and who doesn't.

Challenging times let you see what your key team members are really made of. Under pressure the weak snap, the fickle desert, the meek crumble but the loyal superstars within your team continue to shine like a beacon. Pay extra close attention to your team in true tribulations and you will learn all that you will ever need to know about them.

Loyalty is a reciprocal kind of thing. You can't expect to get any unless you give loads out. Loyal leaders build loyal teams. Loyal teams rule. In an increasingly transient world a little old-fashioned loyalty goes a hell of a long way.

Loyalty between team members, customers and suppliers are all pivotal to long-term growth.

Building a reciprocal loyalty within your team fosters your culture. And in turn helps you weather the harshest of blizzards on the tundra.

IF YOUR VENTURE STANDS
A CHANCE OF BECOMING TRULY,
ABSOLUTELY AWESOME THEN
IT WILL BE THROUGH
STELLAR LEADERSHIP AND
NOT MANAGERIAL ACUMEN.

SHIPS NEED CAPTAINS

'Here's to the crazy ones. The misfits. The rebels. The troublemakers.
The round pegs in the square holes. The ones who see things differently
. . . While some may see them as the crazy ones, we see genius.
Because the ones who are crazy enough to think that they can change
the world, are the ones who do.'
Steve Jobs (business punk)

If your venture stands a chance of becoming truly, absolutely awesome then it will be through stellar leadership and not managerial acumen. Competent managers are ubiquitous and average companies are overloaded with them. Having great leaders in your team can help you change the world. The founders and the leaders throughout your business need to:

1/ Give People Goosebumps

Without a vision, today's beautiful dream will be transmogrified into tomorrow's insane nightmare.

With vision there will be no stopping you. Supersize it. The bigger, the more ambitious, the more outlandish, the better.

Ambitious leaders need to sell the challenge, frame it in reality, tell it how it is, and sell it like it isn't. Making it crazily ambitious, whilst simultaneously making it almost within reach. They need to encourage their team to believe in it, and concurrently ensure they are rabidly hungry to achieve it.

Whatever it is, you better make sure the vision is one shiny mother. It needs to be stratospherically awesome and totally compelling. Unless it gives everyone goosebumps go back to the drawing board. You need your team to sign up in blood. Feed their hearts and stimulate their souls. Paint a picture of a world that does not yet exist.

In the country of the blind the one-eyed man is king. Eye up, mother-fucker.

2/ Celebrate Like a Nutter

We all feel good when what we're doing is recognized and valued. It's simple stuff, but believe me it can make a world of difference. If you want your team to really rumble you'll need to recognize their efforts. Explicitly and frequently. Leave your heartfelt praise and encouragement ringing in their ears and the impact can be off the charts.

If someone kicks a field goal, celebrate it. Whoop it up. And chances are they'll kick a little harder, further and faster next time.

Contextualize the recognition, let them know how they've helped the over-arching mission. The most important and motivational praise and recognition ties the employee's actions back into the framework of the company so they know just how significant their contribution is in making the overall vision a reality.

3/ Give Time

What's the single most important thing you can give your team? The International System of Quantities. Or 'time' to you and me. It's easy to give other stuff, but your time is indeed a special gift. And your team knows that. So when you give it, it is received as the most precious of favours.

The more time you give, the more time you get. Folk will be inspired to go the extra mile for you if you put in the miles for them. Time is a most valuable asset: time over diamonds, baby.

If you are going to spend time on anything, spend it on your team. This is the most important thing that real leaders can spend their time on. If you don't give enough time to your team, then your ship won't have a captain and ships without captains go nowhere.

4/ Be the Safety Net

The Business Big Top is both a fun and a dangerous place. Full of clowns, freaks, high rollers, raging beasts and the occasional bearded lady. Protect your team at all costs and be the safety net. Be a buffer. They need to know you are the alpha male or matriarch looking out for them. Take the heat, take the hit, take the fall, do whatever it takes. Become a crash-test dummy. Buckle up. The buck stops with you.

Build reciprocal trust. This is like rocket fuel for growth. Folk perform when they feel comfortable, safe and secure. When they know their leader is looking out for them. When they know their leader will stand up for them and protect them if something goes wrong. Your team is your business, your growth and your future, look out for it.

IF YOU ARE GOING TO
SPEND TIME ON ANYTHING,
SPEND IT ON YOUR TEAM.

5/ Add Great People to the Team

As a leader your hiring decisions will define your team and they will define you.

Unless you add amazing people to your team, you are going to spend a hell of a lot of time trying to get average people to consistently make great decisions. The crux of business is basically either trying to force idiots to make intelligent decisions through frameworks or systems, or hiring exceptional people capable of making intelligent decisions in the first place. Obviously the latter looks more attractive, but finding exceptional people is like trying to find a needle in a giant stack of idiot needles.

Think of yourself as the overlord. Only you can protect your team by establishing and enforcing entry standards and by making sure freshers will not endanger the culture you are building. One hammerhead appointment might rip through your business like a virus. As leader you get to decide who makes the cut and who doesn't. Great leaders earn respect by only adding the best.

Adding poor people to a finely tuned team has a massive effect on that team's morale and on their performance. Alpha dogs want to work with alpha dogs, so you have a responsibility to only add alphas to your already A-list teams. Teams tend to operate at, or close to, the ability level of the weakest team member.

Great leaders have a knack of adding exceptional people to their teams. Companies live and die by how good their hiring decisions are. Hire too many idiots and you will become one yourself.

6/ Take Ownership

A great leader takes complete ownership. Poor decisions made by people within your team are a wake-up call and a reflection of your own ability, or should I say inability, as leader. Whatever happens, good, bad or ugly, it is a direct consequence of your leadership.

Blame cultures are for philistines and military hardware freaks. When things go wrong (and they will) poor leaders are quick to pass the buck. It wasn't me, it was him; well, listen up – it was you. Good leaders understand that ultimately all decisions are a reflection of their own leadership skills. Bad call equals bad leader. Great leaders also quickly use these situations as a personal development opportunity to provide constructive feedback. This will ensure the team understands how they could have made a better decision, which will massively increase the likelihood of them making better decisions in the future.

The best captains take full responsibility for every outcome whilst engaging, equipping and empowering their crews to make consistently brilliant decisions. Empowerment without responsibility leads to anarchy. Empowerment with responsibility leads to everyone in the business acting like leaders and stepping up to the plate.

Leaders are rare inspirational beings. Managers are ten a penny; the world is full of adequately competent middle managers trapped in corporate hell. Unless you're happy with the status quo, avoid them like they have the plague. True leaders are exceptional and their impact can be stratospheric.

Hold fast and keep the faith.

THE GOOD
BREWDOG

THE BREWDOG CHARTER

Most companies' core values, if they have such a thing, suck. The same meaningless cobbled-together crap put together by a consultancy firm who don't give a damn about their own culture, let alone anyone else's. Respect, ethics, responsibility, blah, blah, blah: a long-winded cocktail of statements which either should go without saying or have been thrown around so often they have lost any semblance of relevance.

At BrewDog we always like to do things ourselves and we always like to do things differently. We were over seven years old (which is forty-nine in dog years) before we felt the need to expressly articulate our BrewDog Charter. Up until that point it was completely intuitive. The company was small enough so that everyone instantly knew what was important to us and how we love to do things and this flowed from Martin and me leading by example down through our teams. We felt it was stupid to articulate something everyone already knew anyway.

However, with over 400 new people due to join our team in 2016 and with teams now at over fifty locations globally, we recently decided it was time to articulate what being BrewDog was all about as we look to not only protect but enhance our company culture as we continue our rapid growth.

The process was collaborative. Starting off with a team survey of over 400 BrewDog pups we then distilled the sentiments down through a tight focus group of twenty of our most long-standing employees. We all pretty much knew what the values were going to be because everyone at BrewDog is very clear about what we care about and how we do things. This is our charter:

THE BREWDOG CHARTER

WE ARE ON A MISSION TO MAKE OTHER PEOPLE AS PASSIONATE
ABOUT GREAT CRAFT BEER AS WE ARE.

WE BLEED CRAFT BEER

THIS IS OUR TRUE NORTH.

WE ARE UNCOMPROMISING

IF WE DON'T LOVE IT, WE DON'T DO IT. EVER.

WE BLOW SHIT UP

WE ARE AMBITIOUS. WE ARE RELENTLESS. WE TAKE RISKS.

WE ARE GEEKS

LEARN OBSESSIVELY. SHARE EVANGELICALLY.

WITHOUT US, WE ARE NOTHING

WE ARE BREWDOG.

Our charter is our moral compass. The fact that it was created by
the people who live these values daily gives it much more power and
weight as our team members can take complete ownership of the type
of culture we are looking to continue building. The new charter acts as
the rudder on the good ship *BrewDog*.

SECTION F:
VELOCITY, TIME AND SPACE FOR DEDICATED LIBERTINES

Hello, here goes. Buckle up and hold on tight. This is the ultimate white-knuckle ride. This section contains ideas, philosophies, mindsets and rules to help you distort space and time to ensure you achieve your aims. Speed is essential for the business punk – that's you, so you'd better sit up and pay attention.

You will need to relentlessly drive your business forward. If you stop striving to improve and grow even for a second, you become a sitting duck and our harsh world will quickly turn you from a feathery friend into a feet-up floater. You don't just need to move, you need to be able to move faster than anyone else.

All the ideas here are road-tested. All with plenty of miles left on the clock and all with a tank full with gas. They have all been put into practice and the practice hammered out there on the circuit.

Time, for a young hungry twenty-first-century business punk, is money – literally. Too much downtime and there will be a downturn in your prospects. Your time management needs to be ruthless and you need to squeeze more out of time. Seconds rapidly vaporize into months.

Stellar time management is a key advantage for a new business. When you're cash poor and time poor you have to think differently, faster and smarter than the competition. They have decades of experience (which, by the way, counts for zip), a legion of minions, a galaxy of time and gold in the bank.

In this section we will analyse how to maximize your time, as well as outlining how the competition wastes theirs. We will detail some simple things you can do to stack the odds firmly in your favour when it comes to creativity and proactivity. Running a growing business you will need to be a delusional schizophrenic, switching hats faster than the Mad Hatter himself, as you go from solving problems one minute to searching for inspiration the next.

Speed is pivotal, but along with speed comes bedlam. However, without a healthy dose of chaos, life (and business) just become far too pedestrian and boring. As a small start-up you have a hell of a lot of catching up to do with a superfluity of mature companies and the best way to do that is through being efficient with your own time and with your company's time.

You will need to move fast, break rules, blow up everything in your path and take everything by the scruff of the neck. You need to be your own hero.

Fasten your seat belts, hold on tight, drop a gear and hit the turbos.

CREATE CREATIVE SPACE

'Nothing vast enters the life of mortals without a curse.'
Sophocles (tragedian punk)

He might not have known it at the time (he died in 406 BC) but this ancient Greek writer was talking about smartphones, emails, the internet and the constant brain-dead state their overbearing influence has on their victims. People today are pretty much all like foie gras goose zombies – stuffed so full of pointless information from every quarter that they are bloated, terrified, yet simultaneously numb and comatose.

If you, like many people today, exist in this state, you will never achieve anything meaningful, ever. If you live your life glued to a smartphone, tweeting every five minutes, reading emails and loading images of yourself on to Facebook you should skip this chapter, and perhaps the whole book.

To create something meaningful, you need to first create some headspace. Creative space to allow your ideas to germinate, grow and flourish. Work harder, think smarter and focus with laser-like efficiency.

If you are just concerned with the here and now, then you'll stay in this spoon-fed world. Creativity is about the next big thing, not the last. Help to make your venture future-proof. You need to ensure your creativity and imagination are not suffocated and stifled by perpetual connection. Thoughts need room to develop; you kill them if you fill empty spaces by being umbilically tethered to your devices.

You simply cannot imagine what will be if you are constantly concerned with what already is. You have to be ruthless and create an environment completely free from background noise and distractions and spend as much time in this space as possible. Lock the door, switch off the phone, switch off the computer, wear noise-cancelling headphones. Block everything out.

Create your own space and let it rip. A device-free zone, no distractions, no interruptions, just you and your ideas. A mecca of thought, where you worship daily. This is essential. Take the time and reap the benefits. Be creative, be proactive, be different.

CREATIVITY IS ABOUT THE NEXT BIG THING, NOT THE LAST.

Make the time to develop the ideas that will have the biggest impact on your enterprise, and, in turn, on your bottom line. Be disciplined. Ruthlessly adhere to daily creative sessions.

Make the time, make the space. Otherwise the only thing you'll be thinking about is where your next pay cheque is coming from.

I have two desks in my office. One digital and one analogue. My digital desk has my computer, my phone, my mobile phone, and is where I can be fully connected to the world if I want to be. It is also where I can be fully connected to my devices but not connected to the outside world if I so choose. My analogue desk has notepads, big blank sheets of paper, pens, pencils and nothing else.

The clear distinction between the two workspaces lets my head get into the proper zone for the type of work I am about to do. If I need to be in the zone and just crunch out some emails, I take my post at my digital desk. If I need to design the launch campaign for a new beer, review new design work, analyse finances or put a presentation together for a team meeting, then I am rocking it old-school at my analogue desk where my brain can really click into gear, free from digital distractions. I do my best work on my analogue desk.

I also try to spend as much time as possible away from both desks, away from my office and out in the real world. Few revolutions are started from behind a desk.

BE CREATIVE, BE PROACTIVE,

BE DIFFERENT.

GET ON THE OFFENSIVE

Being proactive helps you to build a great business. Being reactive means you'll have a failing business. Proactive equals success. Reactive equals a one-way bus ticket to Loserville.

Today it is all too easy to fall into the reactionary workflow trap. The fact that you are almost always contactable by a host of methods means that the potential for wicked little vortexes of reactionary workflows is off the charts. Reacting to the reaction soon becomes the actual work and you are heading nowhere at all.

A reactionary workflow is a self-imposed and destructive vicious cycle. And this is a catastrophic carousel which far too many businesses are caught in. Pecking away at inboxes, incoming calls, messages and social-media feeds just to stay afloat, whilst the important tasks get neglected because people are too 'busy' without ever stopping to question what they are actually 'busy' doing.

The inherent truism is that the more reactionary workflow you indulge in, the more reactionary workflow you create. A self-fulfilling prophecy which, as it compounds, sucks you down a desperate sinkhole as you completely lose sight of what really matters. If you start down the reactionary road, you pick up speed at an alarming rate.

Being reactive is addictive. People get addicted to how busy they look. Reactionary workflows are the workplace equivalent to heroin: savagely addictive and deadly. Jam on the anchors, put it in low and take the next exit, and breathe.

If you are caught in the reactionary then all you are doing is dealing with things which have already happened. However, to really make an impact with your business you need to be much more concerned with what is going to happen. You need to create the time and space to be proactive if you want to create the future.

Being proactive means taking a step back from the day-to-day hustle and bustle. Being proactive means creating headspace and creating a creative space. Being proactive means taking time to work on the business rather than in the business. Being proactive means trusting your team to run the business as you focus on driving it forward. Being proactive in a quickly growing small company can be the hardest thing in the world to do. But you simply have to do it.

At BrewDog we have a fifty-fifty rule for our five directors. I and the other four people who lead our business are only allowed to spend half of our time working on the day-to-day operations of the company, on solving current challenges and dealing with existing issues and we have to spend at least half of our time working on ways to improve, grow and develop our business, on ways to drive us towards our next phase of growth. If we were not ruthlessly self-disciplined with this, if we did not stick to this principle with verve and vigour, then we would all too easily get swamped and sucked into the daily grind and our growth would pretty much grind to a halt.

If you are leading a company, organization or a team, then don't feel like you have to get back to everyone instantly, or even that quickly. It is much better to disappoint a few people over some small things than to give up working on the vital things, the big-picture things, the change-the-world things. Screw the illusion of professionalism, leave that to the lawyers and the accountants of this world. It's easy to answer emails – some folks spend their lives doing it – it is much harder to sit down and be original.

I only respond to emails every two days. This helps create the space I need to be proactive. Here is my auto response:

Hello,

Thanks for the email. To better respond to the needs of our rapidly growing business I will only be responding to emails every second day. Between looking after our awesome customers, building a new brewery, developing our team and opening craft-beer bars, things have got kinda busy.

If you would like a quicker response, one of our team will be able to help you. http://www.brewdog.com/contact

And don't worry if I don't reply. I will have read the email and I will follow up if required. Just doing my bit to break the email chain and save the planet (or something like that).

Less emails should equate to more productivity, more brewing of awesome beers and more time to eat sandwiches.

Walk tall, kick ass and learn to speak craft beer,
J

Be proactive. Make the space, make the time. You need to guard your space like a lioness protecting her cubs. Guard it ferociously and use it wisely. Being informed and connected is a disadvantage when it steals your time to think and make a real difference. Build a team and structure that allows you to flex. That allows you the space and the time to be proactive.

And here is the crux: firstly, being proactive gives you the time and perspective to see things up ahead, to scan the horizon. This allows you to spot potential issues and fix them before they become issues. Secondly, being proactive also allows you to build structures and teams which will help ensure the business operates more smoothly. Both of these combine to reduce the amount of reactionary work created within the business. So by being proactive you reduce the volume of reactionary workflow, which in turn creates more time to be pro-active. You need to be strong enough to break the cycle.

Distracting opportunities (which are not really opportunities) and reactionary workflows have to die in order for your crusade and more important projects to truly come to life.

Busy fool or make a difference? It's your call. Decide now, later is too late.

BEING INFORMED AND
CONNECTED IS A DISADVANTAGE
WHEN IT STEALS YOUR
TIME TO THINK AND MAKE
A REAL DIFFERENCE.

STEAL AND BASTARDIZE

'A punk is someone who knows how to ask the world uncomfortable questions and does everything possible to make sure the world can't cop out of answering those questions. A punk is a person who lives and breathes astonishment. Astonishing other people and astonishing yourself – that's what art is for us, and without art, life can't exist. It would be too boring.'
Pussy Riot (new wave Russian punks)

Creative people need inspiration. And they find it in the weirdest places: books, films, galleries, cities, architecture, shops, photos, poems, eavesdropping, random conversations. Inspiration is literally everywhere; it's just a matter of tuning in to it. If you can't find inspiration in everything you look at, then you are not looking hard enough. Buy it, beg it, borrow it – who gives a damn, just make sure you get it. Then deconstruct it, obsess over it, re-engineer it, recycle it, and turn it into something new.

And for the cherry on the inspiration cake – figure out how to apply it to your own business and your crusade.

David Bowie or was it David Jones or was it Ziggy Stardust? Anyway, some bloke with orange hair said, 'The only art I'll ever study is stuff I can steal from.' He must have got the idea for those skintight sequinned creations from somewhere. Right?

Look for inspiration everywhere. The only place you should never look is within your own industry. Screw what all the other clowns are doing. Ignore it, blank it out; it is of no relevance or significance whatsoever. You don't want to follow the pack, you need to lead from the front. Go your own way and create your own trend. Looking at what other people are doing in your industry is a replacement for thinking for yourself. It is also a sure-fire way to be, at best, second rate.

Take time to be bored. Creative people need time doing nothing. Creativity is like snail baiting, it can't be rushed. Give yourself time and space, wander round your house in your socks, naked, in women's clothes, in men's clothes. I don't give a damn – just do whatever it takes to come up with the goods. Give yourself time for rejuvenation and renewal. Be obsessive, be compulsive about the things you love and give birth to an obsessively compulsive masterpiece.

You also need to do things which scare the hell out of you. Regularly. I find I am at my sharpest and best when everything is on the line. Blitzing yourself with adrenalin is an underutilized business strategy. As a management team Martin and I have held meetings whilst diving with killer whales in Norway, whilst racing dune buggies in Mexico and whilst ice diving in Michigan. You need to constantly challenge yourself to embrace new cultures, perspectives and challenges.

Few great concepts come from a comfortable place. Create an uncomfortable zone. Think outside what you know and understand. Comfort zones are places where average people do mediocre things. As soon as your brain is comfortable it takes the rest of the day off. Your head can get all too comfortable in its routine and daily surroundings. You need to make it uncomfortable and to embrace new perspectives and difficult challenges. So change your environment, stimulate the grey matter and make it matter. Spend time getting inspiration and pushing yourself out of your comfort zone. You will like the results.

Each day is a brand-new canvas. *Carpe diem.*

COMFORT ZONES ARE PLACES
WHERE AVERAGE PEOPLE
DO MEDIOCRE THINGS.

EMPIRES ARE BUILT THROUGH LEAPS OF FAITH

Keep moving. If anyone says stop, screw them – they know nothing – keep going. You have to keep moving and keep moving at a pace. Unless you are moving, you have no idea what path you should be on.

Action creates clarity, proactivity reveals strategy, and moving unveils the path. Remember that bit in *Indiana Jones and the Last Crusade* where Jones (an antique-hunting punk) needs to take a leap of faith and step on to an invisible bridge over a colossal canyon? Indy's path is seemingly blocked; he can't go back and he can't go forward as to go forward would mean plummeting into the abyss. The only exit is death, or so thought the cinema-going audience of the 1980s. He has to take a bold step out into the unknown. He has no option but to act, with nothing at all but his own faith to secure his future. He steps out, the audience trembles, Indy grimaces and as he lands a bridge emerges to the other side. He did not know what was going to happen, but he took the big leap of faith anyway.

What is true for a fictional 1930s hero is true for a twenty-first-century business. You will need to take big leaps into the unknown with faith, confidence and a machete.

Taking a leap of faith does two main things: firstly, it provides clarity as to what further actions you should take and, secondly, it creates further action. *You need to create a culture of action and a culture of moving fast within your business.*

We constantly do things at BrewDog with no idea at all if they are going to work out or how they could potentially play out. We don't wait for perfect solutions, we don't conduct research, we just do what we feel is right and then believe in our ability as a team to make it work. By actually taking action, we get the clarity needed to take further action. This creates an ever accelerating cyclone of activity which drives our business forward.

Reality reigns supreme. All the analysis, presumption and conjecture in the world is a poor and distant relative to reality. Not moving forward, not taking a bold leap of faith into the unknown completely puts the brakes on your enterprise, and extends the time frame between the idea and the all-valuable real-world insights being obtained.

You will not always get it right. But every time you move, every time you make a bold decision, it will take you one step closer to finding the path you are searching for. The absolute worst thing you can do is nothing.

In *The Matrix* Neo did not know he was the one until his actions made him the one. He had to take a leap of faith. Your actions will determine your destiny. If you don't move, and move with speed and purpose, the path will never be unveiled to you. If you don't move, you will never have an epiphany where you see the road map for your enterprise glowing inside your spinning mind.

Act, assess, refine, repeat. And repeat. And repeat. And repeat. A shot in the dark is still a shot.

THE ABSOLUTE WORST THING YOU CAN DO IS NOTHING.

ACT FIRST, THINK LATER

You can 'what if' yourself to death. Treating an uncertain world as if it is predictable is for charlatans. Long-term planning is just a waste of resources and brain power. The surest route to catastrophic failure is not to act and not to take any risks.

At BrewDog a lot of our biggest successes came off the back of a radical and rapid change of strategy following various big gambles. Back in 2008 we started exporting, which was a big leap into the unknown for us, and contrary to what everyone told us we also started shipping draught beer in our own kegs to export markets. This was a disaster. We lost so many of our kegs and the ones that did make it back took almost a year to come home. On the upside we discovered there actually was a huge appetite for our draught beer internationally. Through this debacle we were forced to find a much better solution and we pioneered a one-way recyclable keg, becoming the first UK brewery to use KeyKegs. We now send over 5,000 of these kegs overseas per month and this is a significant part of our business, which only came about because we dived in with two feet initially, without having any idea what would actually happen.

When we first started making ice beers we did not wait until we had the theory all worked out, we just jumped in and did it. Freezing our beers in a local ice-cream factory's cold store before eventually retrofitting a refrigerated shipping container for our purposes. We constantly refined the method through trial and error as opposed to calculations and models. Within months we were famous for making the strongest and most exciting ice beers in the world. If we had waited for a perfect solution, we would still be waiting. We just dived in and made it happen. Then we refined it, dived in again and then made it happen even better.

Shoot first, ask questions later, and take no prisoners. Act fast and think afterwards. Your strategy must exist within the over-arching framework of your mission. It must be crystallized, polished and fine-tuned from real actions that you and your team take. Take the initiative, do something, do anything, just keep rolling. You simply cannot wait for perfect solutions. You need to be a dogmatic pragmatist. Embrace the realpolitik ethos. Decide and move.

We now have over forty BrewDog bars worldwide. But if we had not taken the huge gamble and opened our first one in Aberdeen in 2010, we would not have any of them. We had no idea what we were doing, we had never run a bar before, we just believed in the concept and bet heavily on our own ability to make it work.

That decision opened the floodgates for a tidal wave of activity and expansion. The more action you take, the more opportunities open themselves up to you. Action flows from action. Nothing flows from nothing.

So, you need to take action. But make sure you take account of all the other bits of guidance in this book with the actions you are taking. It needs to be intelligent, leveraged, well negotiated, informed action with a firm grip of your finances, company culture and product quality. And it needs to be fast and furious.

You can't let the presence of risk stop you from taking action. There will always be risk. And there should always be risk. BrewDog has succeeded to date because we were callously indifferent to risk and mortally adverse to staying still.

The best way to prepare for the future is to create it.

GO FAST OR GO HOME

Some folks think slow is good. We believe fast is better. Speed changes everything. Fast-forward to tomorrow and there will be two types of business: the fast and the dead.

Speed is a game changer. Being able to move at high velocity is essential. Whilst others are deliberating, you're out of the blocks, accelerating at light speed. The competitive advantage of being flexible and able to do things at rapid pace cannot be overstated. Most companies are overly bureaucratic, the decision-making process is laboured and cumbersome. Being agile and responsive gives you the edge. Speed is key: it is one of your greatest weapons in your arsenal to change the world.

At BrewDog we have always taken a blitzkrieg approach to business. We've built ours on informed decisions, implemented faster than a jackrabbit on speed. For the last four years we have been the fastest-growing business in the UK.

Speed is contagious. You need to build it into every aspect of everything you do. It needs to be ingrained into your team and your extended network. Your suppliers and partners need to be lightning fast too. Moving at your speed, not theirs. If they can't keep the pace, replace them with ones who can. You need to set the pace your business moves at; you can't let others dictate this to you.

We have a few bits of data which we use at BrewDog to show the importance of speed to our teams.

THIS CHART SHOWS OUR GROWTH OVER THE FIRST
SEVEN YEARS COMPARED TO SOME
OF OUR FASTEST-GROWING INDUSTRY PEERS:

	FOUNDED	YEAR 7 (HECTOLITRES BREWED)	BARS	GROWTH (TIMES SLOWER THAN BREWDOG)
BREWDOG	2007	89,000	25	0
BREWERY A	1994	21,500	1	7.1
BREWERY B	1980	19,000	1	7.7
BREWERY C	2000	8,000	1	18.2
INDUSTRY AVERAGE	VARIABLE	4,000	0	36

Brewery A and Brewery B are two of the largest and fastest-growing breweries in America, and Brewery C is one of the fastest growing in the UK. At BrewDog our growth has been pretty remarkable, especially when you put it into perspective. And it is when you put it into perspective that we can precisely articulate the importance of speed.

We have grown over seven times faster than Brewery A and Brewery B and over eighteen times faster than Brewery C. That means if we can save a week on a project then we save seven weeks on our fastest-moving counterpart, Brewery A, but a remarkable thirty-six-week march on our industry overall. Compared to our fastest-growing UK industry peer, if we can save a week, we can steal an eighteen-week head start on them. If we can save a day on a project, we are essentially saving over seven weeks on the rest of the industry. And if we can pull something a month forward, then we save three years of industry-average time. Meaning that even one day is worth scrambling for.

Another metric we use to ingrain the importance of speed in our business is a quick bit of overhead analysis. Overheads were not too much of an issue for us when we started; as long as Martin and I could feed ourselves and our pup we were pretty much happy. Now with a team of over 400 and over fifty business locations our overheads are much larger than a few sandwiches, a £400 monthly cheque to the council and some dog biscuits. Between wages, rent, utilities, insurances and finance charges our overheads are now over £100,000 per working day.

This daily overhead bill needs to be allocated across all the projects and undertakings we have as a business. So, if we can make something happen a day earlier we can save a percentage of £100,000 of our overheads. If we can make something happen a week quicker, we save a percentage of £500,000, and if we can make a project happen a month earlier, if we can pull a delivery date from a supplier forward by a month or if we can launch a new product or a new bar a month earlier we save a percentage of £2m. And all of these savings can be invested back into the things which are important to us – our people and our beers.

At BrewDog we constantly leverage everything in our power to make all of our projects happen as quickly as possible and consequently we steal a march on an entire industry and save a bucketload of cash to boot.

> YOU NEED TO SET THE PACE
> YOUR BUSINESS MOVES AT;
> YOU CAN'T LET OTHERS
> DICTATE THIS TO YOU.

Moving at pace allows you to identify and take advantage of opportunities your competitors aren't even aware of. It enables you to test ideas, and for those ideas to be shaped by tangible insights rather than guesswork. The world around us flexes and changes at an ever increasing pace. The businesses and organizations that are going to stay relevant are the ones which can move fast enough not only to stay in touch, but to get ahead.

A fast reactive business creates a high-energy environment, the type of environment needed to retain talented, like-minded people. Being agile, lean and manoeuvrable as a business is the future. And on the occasions you get it wrong, and there will be a few, you can move very quickly to get it right.

You need to be much less afraid of making mistakes than you are of missing opportunities because you went too slowly.

Screw down the throttle and hammer it flat out through the twists and turns. Slow is boring. Slow is dead. Slow is irrelevant. Be fast.

MOVING AT PACE ALLOWS YOU TO IDENTIFY AND TAKE ADVANTAGE OF OPPORTUNITIES YOUR COMPETITORS AREN'T EVEN AWARE OF.

GET FORGIVENESS, NOT PERMISSION

To hell with permission, absolve your sins with forgiveness. We run our business and live our lives by this mantra. You should take it for a test drive. There is no warranty, but I guarantee it is the best fun you'll ever have. And it really kicks some ass.

We did not get permission to use an image of Vladimir Putin on our labels. We did not get permission to drive a tank through the streets of central London. We did not get permission to project a 150-feet-high image of Martin and myself, naked, on to the Houses of Parliament. We did not get permission to parachute taxidermic cats out of a helicopter over London. But we did all of these things anyway, and we only almost got arrested twice.

Put your conscience and morals in a drawer, lock it, throw away the key and join the revolution. Because at a certain point you'll have to do things you know you shouldn't. We certainly did. By doing so we were able to grow our business, employ more people and contribute much more to the economy. If a two-bit penny-pushing bureaucratic monkey is going to mess with you, particularly when you're trying to kick-start your local economy and employ people, just hang them out to dry. *Aeternum vale*, monkey.

So jump in with both feet and join the progressive business movement. Waiting for permission will be like waiting for ever. And for ever is a long time. If you have the ambition, then have the balls and go for it.

When we reached our fourth birthday we had outgrown our Fraserburgh brewery's premises. To keep pace with demand we had to think fast and act faster. So we went ahead and installed some giant 200-hectolitre tanks (that's around 50,000 bottles of pure fermented awesomeness in each) on the exterior of our building. Why stop at one when there was room for six. We didn't ask, we didn't wait, we just did. Planning permission would have taken at least six months and would inevitably come with onerous terms and conditions. In that time we would have lost valuable contracts and more importantly valuable time. And waiting would have damaged our long-term growth potential. And guess what? There was no way on this planet that we would let that happen.

Predictably the local pen-pushing authority went ballistic. I pleaded insanity (ignorance actually) as the stand-off turned into stand-down, and finally ran out of steam. They lost their bottle, but we didn't lose any of ours. And if they had tried to remove them, they would have taken a beer suffragette with them – me chained to the tanks in my underpants.

So treat rules, regulations and bureaucrats with the callous indifference they deserve. Focus on what you need to do, and when you need to do it by. Don't wait for anyone or anything. Waiting is for trains, buses and ambitionless wimps. Business needs to roll and keep rolling. Grow your business, employ folk, exonerate your business and vindicate yourself.

There is, however, a subtlety here. This strategy is not quite as risky and reckless as it sounds. I am not advocating gung-ho uncontrolled lawlessness for the sake of it. You need to know how to play the game by the rules and know exactly how the rules work to even consider breaking them. You need to know precisely which rules you can break and which rules you can't. The time to get forgiveness rather than permission is when the consequences for not getting permission are far worse than the consequences for your business of not taking immediate action. Or when you believe you will be able to game-face it up and dodge the consequences.

The not-asking-for-permission philosophy also extends to your team. Your team should be governed by your values and your culture and not by policies and rules. They should be empowered and have the autonomy to do their jobs and not have to ask for permission to make and implement decisions to drive the business forward.

Just because you are not supposed to do something does not always mean you shouldn't. Don't let stuffy bureaucratic zombies in cheap suits rule your world. The consequences of not getting permission to do something are almost never as bad as you think. So find out what they are and then burn it to the ground.

Not asking for permission is not just a business strategy but also a way of life. It's not about abusing situations but about knowing when to push the boundaries. It's about realizing that the overwhelming number of people in life are naysayers and sometimes you gotta just roll the dice and say to hell with the consequences.

DON'T LET STUFFY BUREAUCRATIC ZOMBIES IN CHEAP SUITS RULE YOUR WORLD.

THE NEW CHAOS THEORY

'*Chaos is inherent in all compounded things. Strive on with diligence.*'
Buddha (happy punk)

Welcome to bedlam, take a seat, we'll be with you in a moment. If you want fast growth, buckle up for some chaos theory. Chaos is your amigo in the roller coaster to making it. It's a constant. And if it isn't, start worrying. If you don't have a healthy amount of disorder and internal mayhem, then you are not pushing hard enough. So push harder. Anarchy and pandemonium will be your co-pilots in this crazy journey.

Fast-track growth means you're constantly in flux. Every change to your business is a jump into the unknown. One small step for you, one giant leap for your business. New people, new partners, new systems, new markets, new products, new premises and new customers. It is a never-ending Ferris wheel of things which fundamentally change everything you do and how you do it.

Your team should be in a spin, out of control but in reach of the joystick. Like space monkeys on steroids.

CHAOS IS ADDICTIVE.

At BrewDog we eat space monkeys for breakfast. We thrive on chaos; it is our modus operandi. We have become so used to the constant state of flux that our growth creates that it is hauntingly disconcerting when we do occasionally and briefly feel on top of things. Thankfully this never lasts long; we quickly enter the next asteroid assault, and anarchy prevails.

In the last twelve months we have opened fifteen new bars, launched the world's most ambitious crowdfunding campaign, built a new £25m brewery, launched sixty new beers, added 350 new team members, installed a new business operational software system and added over 10,000 new customers all over the world. Oh, and started building a new brewery in America. For us, the chaos is addictive.

We are used to living with chaos in our business, and over the years we have learned there are certain things you need to do in order to ensure that the environment is energetic, empowered and proactive and does not descend into disillusioned haphazard ochlocracy. And those things revolve around an intense focus on the three pillars, especially on people and company culture.

Firstly, you need to build speed and an acceptance of chaos into your company culture and ensure you hire the type of people that can handle a fast-paced, hectic and occasionally unruly environment.

Secondly, communication is completely pivotal and it will be the glue that just about manages to hold everything together during periods of intense growth. Without great communication a healthy level of chaos quickly descends into turmoil and disarray. You need to keep the team as well informed as possible so they can buy into the excitement of what the business is both planning and currently achieving, both of which act as a great motivator. Through regular updates everyone can be informed and aligned as you form a united front whilst sailing over stormy seas. Your only way to win is as a team. The more you can also acknowledge individual contributions and set them into the context of the overall objective and mission, the more bought in and engaged your team will be.

Thirdly, you need to quickly get into the habit of expanding ahead of the growth curve. Massively oversize everything, add people before you need them, put systems in place before, as opposed to after, they are needed and put an infrastructure in place for where you want to be in two years' time.

And fourthly, you need to look after your finances with the same level of care Captain Hook would use when changing a contact lens. The one place you cannot tolerate chaos is when it comes to the finances of your business. During growth spurts you need to realize that profit is only on paper, and as you grow quickly your working-capital requirements skyrocket. If you can't meet these requirements, it is game over. You also need to be extra diligent in protecting your profit margins. Your gross profits will need to be super-strong in order to fuel the growth and cover the working-capital requirements whilst paying for the expansion ahead of the curve.

In the end chaos is your friend, but never turn your back on it. Chaos should always be in front of you, in plain sight. Inevitably chaos, anarchy and disorder are the everyday reality for any fast-growing company. Learn to live with them, accept them and thrive on them. Your team needs to understand that the closer you fly to the sun, the greater your chances of survival, and the greater the chances of achieving your mission.

IF YOU DON'T HAVE
A HEALTHY AMOUNT OF DISORDER
AND INTERNAL MAYHEM,
THEN YOU ARE NOT
PUSHING HARD ENOUGH.
SO PUSH HARDER.

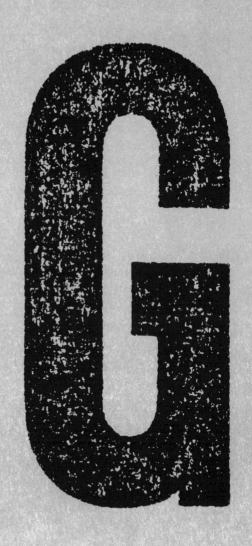

SECTION G:
INSIDE THE HEAD OF A BUSINESS PUNK

'Weakness of attitude becomes weakness of character.'
Albert Einstein (science punk)

All sales are final. 'G' is for Go! This section contains some of the most important philosophies, mindsets, ambitions and rules for the twenty-first-century business punk – that's you, so you'd better sit up and pay attention.

There are hundreds, if not thousands, of business strategies. A hurricane circus that blasts out a never-ending orgy of ideas. Concocted by the brilliant, the mediocre and the insane. The ones I recommend here worked for us.

It's an eclectic mix of original, bastardized, bootlegged and reinvented notions. But they are all tried and tested in the real world. They have all been put into practice and the practice hammered out there on the circuit.

Attitude is everything, for both you and your team. It is the one single thing you can always control so it logically follows that you need to become expert in controlling it.

Loads of potentially catastrophic stuff is going to happen to every single enterprise. It is how you react to it that shapes your destiny and your place in the world. Only morons spend their precious time and energy worrying about things which are completely out of their control. Just focus on what you can control and make sure it is the best it can be.

We've never been risk averse at BrewDog. A modern business can't be. So I stand or fall by this list, and last time I checked we still had a pulse. So read up, load up, kick some ass and reinvent your world.

Time to put yourself on the line, time to live or die for something you believe in. These are the coins of the realm in my world, the keys to the safe and the passwords to survival.

Life's a bitch – step up and skill up or you're going down.

ONLY MORONS SPEND THEIR PRECIOUS TIME AND ENERGY WORRYING ABOUT THINGS WHICH ARE COMPLETELY OUT OF THEIR CONTROL.

CYNICAL OPTIMISM

Things will get tough. Tribulations hit you from every quarter. You will be faced with numerous challenges. Stay resolute and stay optimistic. Stay focused and take all challenges head on. Believe unwaveringly in yourself, your team and your mission.

The key, however, is that this cannot be a blind faith. It cannot be a cartoon brand of cheery optimism. The buoyant confidence cannot seduce you into being optimistically oblivious to real issues. The optimism cannot prevent you fully accepting, recognizing and confronting your biggest challenges on a daily basis. Retaining the belief that you will succeed whilst simultaneously having the self-discipline to confront the cruellest realities of your current status is a formidable combination. Pair buoyant optimism with brutal pragmatism.

So how do you take your challenges out? You don't pump them with a sawn-off shotgun, you make a list. Eh? A list? Yeah – a short one. We take these mothers out five at a time. Write down your five biggest problems, sit down in a room with your team, and solve them. Then on to the next five.

Every week I write a list of our five most pressing challenges and pin it to my wall and stare at it so intently with such a steely determination that I burn it into my retinas. And then I do everything I can to solve the problems. We also have fortnightly management meetings where each member of our management team prepares a list of what they see as our biggest current problems. We never hide. We tackle all our problems head on with a galvanized fortitude. This means we are constantly improving every element of everything we do. No business can afford to stop striving for continual improvement. Focusing with verve and resolve on problems and challenges helps you do just that. Every business, in every sector, will face a plethora of troubles, problems and challenges. A company's success is not defined by how many challenges they face. A company is ultimately defined by how they acknowledge and tackle the obstacles in their way.

Half the trick is to be able to recognize the issues in the first place and the other half of the trick is having the discipline to regularly acknowledge and tackle them. This discipline also develops a knack for recognizing potential issues before they develop into full-blown problems. Identify, prioritize, illuminate and obliterate.

It is all too easy just to focus on the great things (of which there will be plenty) and to sweep all the issues under the carpet. There will be a constant temptation to only focus on the positives, the successes, the wins, the growth. As important as they are, you must not lose sight of the challenges. If you ignore them or are blind to them, they will grow arms, legs, grab a baseball bat and give you and your business a kicking to remember. Just one overlooked issue has the potential to mutate and grow to the point it can easily destroy your business.

By constantly monitoring, and proactively acknowledging the most brutal facts about your current reality, you can find ways to solve them, or better still, turn them into opportunities. You just can't afford to stick your head in the sand. Being blissfully ignorant or wilfully naive is a recipe for business catastrophe.

You need to master a schizophrenic blend of complete confidence in your mission and a totalitarian pragmatic realism when it comes to making sure you always bravely tackle the most pressing and testing issues your business faces. In short, you need to be a cynical optimist.

Keep the faith and front up the issues.

THE PROBLEM IS NEVER THE PROBLEM

'You never change things by fighting the existing reality. To change something, build a new model that makes the existing model obsolete.'
Buckminster Fuller (systems theory punk)

Life isn't easy, and building a successful business is much, much harder. But it should be difficult. If it was easy then everyone would do it and success would not mean anything. Problems are obstacles to overcome on your journey to building an empire. Thousands of problems will hit you broadside over the coming months and years. Jay Z can relate to this. He had exactly ninety-nine problems, excluding his bitch, apparently. As I write this I have thirty-two problems, none of which are bitch-related either.

Solving internal problems quickly and effectively is all about getting to the heart of the why and the what. You need to understand why the problem is happening, and what is causing it. You need to get to the root. If you don't get to the root, it's like using a Band-Aid after being mauled by a lion. Don't deliberate and constantly ponder the effects, get to the root and fix the problem. Load up and give the lion both barrels. Unless you tackle the root cause you are just veiling the symptoms.

External problems need the same approach. Seek out the why and then use all your shiny new negotiating skills to kick its ass. Convince the other party to move the barbed wire as you advance. If you can't get to the why, you'll just be chasing your tail like a crazy dog. Persuade the other party it would be in everyone's interest to change whatever is causing the problem. Remove it, renegotiate it, reinvent it. Do whatever it takes to get the mother off the table.

If you can't get to and change the why which anchors the problem you can never really solve it. And if you can't effectively solve problems, you can't effectively manage and lead your business.

You also need to solve problems and resolve issues quickly. Otherwise they just wear you down. If you were running a marathon, you would not wait until the twenty-second mile to remove a stone from your shoe.

ATTITUDE IS THE DIFFERENCE BETWEEN A SETBACK AND AN ADVENTURE.

A person's attitude towards a problem will tell you so much about that person. You only find out what a person is really like when things get tough, when things go badly wrong or when they are faced with a real problem. As a leader, you should be grateful when things do go wrong or when you are faced with big problems, as these occasions let you see what your team members are truly made of.

Problems only really exist in the minds of people not capable of taking the initiative and making things happen. The best people always see problems as an opportunity to shine, a chance to underline their credentials and show the world just what they are capable of. The problem is never the problem. The real problem is always people's attitude towards the problem.

Attitude is the difference between a setback and an adventure.

CORROBORATION: PROTEST FOR PUNKS

Back in 2011 we wanted to serve the two-thirds pint measure in our craft-beer bars, feeling the size was perfect to showcase some of our stronger, more complex brews. However, due to a 300-year-old licensing law it was illegal to serve beer in this size glass in the UK. We tried writing letters to Parliament and lobbying politicians to no avail. Undeterred we remained determined to get to the source of this problem and resolve it.

We then instigated the world's smallest protest in an attempt to tear-up the stupid laws that say beer can't be served in the two-thirds pint measure. We had a dwarf holding a week-long protest at Westminster, arguing that two thirds of a pint measures should be introduced in British bars. The dwarf had various placards over the course of the week, including **SMALL FOR ALL** and **SIZE MATTERS** and he even got arrested by the police.

However, our tiny protest blew the dust off our archaic licensing laws and brought about the first change to draught-beer measures for over three centuries. Two thirds of a pint is the perfect size for artisanal beers and will help to combat irresponsible drinking as well as introduce new audiences to the craft-beer revolution.

The diminutive remonstration helped us claim another scalp in the form of archaic licensing rules. It was nothing short of a landmark victory for BrewDog. The two-thirds pint measure means British beer drinkers can enjoy bold and creative beers responsibly – we knew that – and we made sure the government caught up.

OUR TINY PROTEST BLEW THE DUST
OFF OUR ARCHAIC LICENSING LAWS
AND BROUGHT ABOUT THE FIRST
CHANGE TO DRAUGHT-BEER MEASURES
FOR OVER THREE CENTURIES.

NETWORKING IS FOR FOOLS

Networking is indeed for fools. High on the illusion of their own self importance. Feeding their fragile egos with lukewarm canapés, cheap champagne and slaps on the back from their fellow fools. Trying desperately to cling to the fantasy that they are not only important and relevant but also somehow gifted merely for being in such an esteemed gathering of fellow fools. Networking events are merely a way for the old, crumbling established order to clutch at the remnants of the rapidly eroding status quo.

Business, and thank goodness for this, is no longer about who you know. It is, quite rightfully, about how good you are. The playing field is now level, the barriers are down, the slimy pimped-up business bourgeoisie no longer hold the keys or the answers. Meaning there is absolutely no reason at all to waste your time networking with them, or anyone else for that matter. Businesses built on networking are destined to fail. They will fail fast and they will fail hard.

Even networking events without the old guard present are a stone-cold waste of time. Wannabes strutting about like they've made it, all trying to appear much smarter, bigger and better than they are. People who specialize in talking a good game but in delivering absolutely nothing. All desperately trying to make everyone in the room feel they are the most successful one there. It is like taking giant egos and throwing them all into the Hadron Collider with some TNT tossed in too for good measure.

So whilst the fools, rats and wannabes are massaging each other's egos you need to be plotting your revenge. Not on them specifically, but on the system that bred such morons. You need to be quietly planning how to blow the status quo to pieces and create a whole new world order. Planning how you can make every single aspect of everything you do better, stronger, faster and more brilliant.

Who you know no longer matters. If you are talented and smart, then people will know about you. Spend your time on improving your own business. Mediocre vol-au-vents are optional.

BUSINESSES BUILT ON NETWORKING ARE DESTINED TO FAIL. THEY WILL FAIL FAST AND THEY WILL FAIL HARD.

MAKE YOUR NOISE COUNT

You need to be a communication genius, or at the very least to have a PhD in it. If you're not a good communicator, let me communicate something to you right now – you are just wasting everyone's time. Unless you are almost at oracle status, you don't have a chance of getting your team aligned, of getting people excited about what you do or of effectively negotiating.

The problem is every mother and his wife thinks they are good at communicating. The reality is very few people really are. Everything you say makes perfect sense in your head; the hard part is ensuring that it makes perfect sense for the person or people you are saying it to as well.

The most important thing is to communicate with clarity, tell it how it is, and tell it in an engaging way. Well over half of all communication is ambiguous. Open the door for ambiguity or misinterpretation and you also let in doubt. Then you really are screwed.

So do the prep, and take the time to deliver top-dollar communication, whatever the medium. You should always imagine the communication from the other party's perspective. Put thought into what you say and how you say it. It might be the most boring bit of advice in this book. However, a leader who ensures what they communicate is precise and unambiguous is a million times more effective than a leader who people only really understand some of the time. Remember, time is money and clarity drives your business forward.

A vital part of communicating is how you do it. Face to face is always best; if not, second best is a phone call. Coming in way down the field and a very poor, distant third is email which just nudges out the carrier pigeon. And if you are going to send an email always make sure you proofread it twice, as well as consider every word from the recipient's perspective. If you don't have time to do that, you don't have time to send the email.

You can build a much stronger bond with someone in a thirty-minute face-to-face meeting, than you can with twelve months of emails. Look into the whites of their eyes and tell them how it is. Build a dialogue and rapport, and you start to build a bond. The stronger the bond, the better the leverage potential you will have.

Email induces jaded lethargy. What email? I didn't get it. They don't get read, they get read incorrectly or deleted. It is a fundamental mistake to think something is done, simply because you sent an email. And it's very easy to take offence from a perfectly harmless and well-meaning email, purely because you are reading it with a perceived tone. So meet people, call people, FaceTime folk or Skype them. Send as few emails as possible. Your enterprise will grow stronger and faster as a result.

It goes without saying, and I know you know, but I'm going to say it anyway. Don't send that damn email. Which one? The one you wrote when steam was coming out of your ears and you were screaming like a banshee. It would be a monumental mistake. It will kill years' worth of trust and goodwill and more often than not will be completely fatal in terms of engagement and morale. Always deal with conflicts and issues calmly and in person. Never by email.

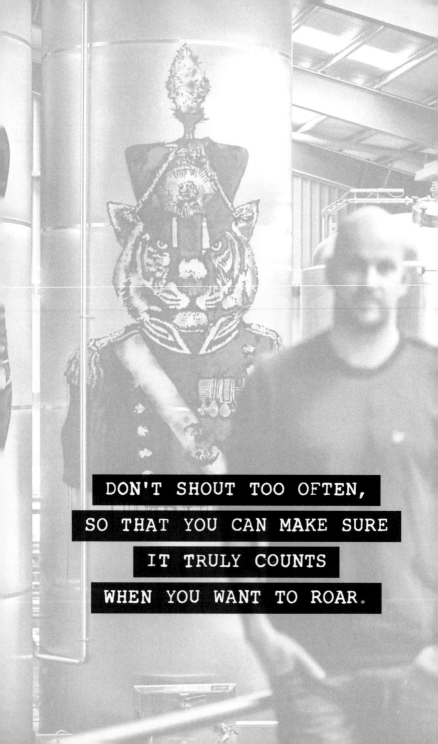

DON'T SHOUT TOO OFTEN,
SO THAT YOU CAN MAKE SURE
IT TRULY COUNTS
WHEN YOU WANT TO ROAR.

MAXIMIZING HUMAN BANDWIDTH

The concept of opportunity cost discussed earlier in the book is also pivotal to the psychology of business. You can only get so much of anyone's attention, so you need to ensure you use it wisely.

You need to apply opportunity cost to people's bandwidth. Everyone has a bandwidth and everyone has far too many things competing for space on their radar. From trade customers to journalists, staff to consumers, your internal infiltration potential is finite. And the more things you try to funnel into their limited bandwidth, the less impact each thing will have as the law of diminishing returns turns into a complete roadblock. It is not so much about the boy who shouted wolf but the boy who shouted new product, new press release, new idea, new feedback until everyone stopped listening. Don't shout too often, so that you can make sure it truly counts when you want to roar.

For instance, every press release you send to journalists has an opportunity cost. There is only so much a journalist will cover a company or a project: the more information you send, the less receptive he or she will be to that information. In the run-up to a big BrewDog release or event we always go quiet for a couple of months to ensure the media is ready and hungry to give our big story maximum exposure. We also limit ourselves to four really big announcements per year.

Customers only have a limited amount of bandwidth for new products. Too many product launches, too many product options simply lead to fatigued and frazzled consumers. We minimize our special-release beers so that we can maximize the impact each one has.

Any feedback, good or bad, you give to your team also comes with opportunity-cost implications. There is only so much praise you can give a team member before it becomes hollow and worthless and there is only so much constructive criticism you can provide before it loses its beneficial component. Don't overwhelm or overload your team with feedback. Instead strategically feed back on the points that are most important to developing your business.

Human opportunity should also dictate your hiring strategy. In a start-up or small company hiring someone, say an accountant, will mean you can't hire someone else, say a driver, a marketer or a logistics controller. You will need to build your team carefully to maximize the impact of each hire.*

Time management is another area where the concept of opportunity cost should be ruthlessly applied. If you are doing something, then it means you can't be doing something else; you need to ensure you use your time in the most important areas.

The time and space you get granted inside someone's consciousness should be cherished like the precious resource it is. Don't waste it like a hammerhead.

* *You should be wary about applying other financial concepts to people. In my experience key team members do not like to be straight line depreciated.*

KEEP YOUR EYES ON THE BALLS

You need targets; you need something to shoot for. You will also need to measure loads of metrics so you are able to know if you are on the right path and instantly be able to ascertain the general health of your business. This is an essential hit list to check off on the way to cosmic domination. Busy fools quickly turn into unemployed ones. If things don't get monitored and measured, then they don't get managed effectively. Fast-paced small companies are crazy places and things frequently slip through the cracks. Just make sure it is not any of the really important stuff by measuring and tracking the fundamentals. Because if you don't, things will bite you like an angry wolf.

When you're shooting for the moon it's easy to take your eye off stuff closer to home. But it is paramount you track at least ten of the most important performance indicators of your business monthly. If you don't, you'll soon be off course, and you won't stand a chance in hell of putting a plan in place to correct your trajectory. And unless you monitor your financials tightly, there's no way on this earth (or any other) to tell if they can support your latest initiative. And you won't see the impact on your business until it's too late. Catch-22.

If something is important to your business – gross margin, the number of customer complaints, staff retention, shipment accuracy, labour ratios, exchange rates, production losses, like-for-like sales growth, sales-to-rent ratios, net profit, EBITDA or a host of other factors – you need to track and monitor it frequently. Do this even when you are tiny and you have just started out and it seems inconsequential; the discipline will stand you in good stead. Once you start monitoring something, then you can start improving it.

As Peter Drucker apparently said, 'What gets measured gets managed.' There is a lot of untapped power in this quote. The simple act of paying close attention to something will cause you to make connections which you never made before, cause you to gain insights which you never before had and help you easily improve things which are crucial to your business.

When it comes to measuring performance, tracking key things and keeping your eyes on the balls, the first step is always monthly management accounts. This will pretty much ensure all of your key financial measures are tracking, locked, loaded and managed. At the most basic level, monthly management accounts give you at least a chance of staying in control of your business. Without them you are already a lost cause. You definitely won't change the world just by doing monthly management accounts, but you sure as hell can't change it if you don't.

Not only do you need monthly management accounts (also known as a monthly P&L statement) you also need to have them within seven days of the end of the month. So many companies wait so long to get these prepared that they can no longer use the information contained therein to help them make effective decisions. When it comes to your management accounts you should definitely be tracking sales, cost of sales, overheads, gross margin, EBITDA and net margin. You will also need to monitor items on your balance sheet at regular and short intervals, such as debtors, creditors and, most importantly, your cash position.

In addition you should track certain other KPIs (key performance indicators), depending on what is important in your business and your current focus. For instance, you should consider tracking things like: average spend per transaction, staff turnover, customer complaints, referrals, shipment accuracy, sales mix, refunds, wastage, sales growth, additional customers, online engagement or staff happiness (to name but a few). In determining which items you need to keep close tabs on it really depends on your business and your objectives.

At BrewDog we put together a monthly pack which has all our financial reporting in the form of our management accounts and balance sheet, along with other key items we track, including like-for-like sales growth in our bars, data on our biggest customers, average value per consignment, staff turnover, average beer scores in our internal tasting panels and brewing data.

Think of it as a health check for your business, and preventative medicine is preferable to emergency surgery. Given over 80% of new businesses fail, the importance of a regular health check cannot be overstated. If you don't measure and track something, you don't have a hope of managing it effectively. Without having up-to-date information at your fingertips you can't make informed life-saving decisions. And you won't have the faintest idea of how to allocate your resources. Life or death – you choose.

No measurement = no reporting = no visibility = no one cares = your ultimate demise. Make sure you measure, control and manage the things which are important to your business's survival.

> **NO MEASUREMENT = NO REPORTING = NO VISIBILITY = NO ONE CARES = YOUR ULTIMATE DEMISE.**

WIN WIN WIN

Negotiate everything like your life depends on it. Your business's life certainly does. The key to negotiating is not merely to make the other party do what you want them to do – all this does is provide short-term gratification to the negotiator. The crux is getting them to want to do what you want them to do, and make them feel like they are getting the deal of the century to boot. Get them hungry for the deal, salivating for it.

Gone are the days of glamorized testosterone-fuelled duels. Locking horns in aggressive head-to-head meetings behind closed doors where the aim was to treat the other negotiating party as a direct opponent and to tear them to shreds. Now the doors are wide open, and in steps the enlightened negotiator. In the modern business, negotiation is the everyday. You will be constantly negotiating with staff, customers, suppliers, partners, designers and lawyers. Everything hinges on your ability to make them as passionate about your business as you are and the success of your venture depends on your ability to make them enthusiastically and purposefully want to do exactly what you want them to.

It should be called convincing, not negotiating. It is really more about persuading and gently, subconsciously coercing than negotiating. And it needs to be a win-win situation for both parties. Cooperation and mutuality in terms of the benefit is the name of the game. There has to be something in it for everyone. If winning isn't mutual you will quickly find yourself renegotiating, this time with a different set of partners.

Always do your negotiation homework. Find out about the other party, what makes them tick, their likes and dislikes. Ultimately think about what's in it for them. Then build your argument around how the deal helps them, because at the end of the day they care much more about what is in their interests than yours.

When it comes to negotiation you need to consider changing the rules of how the game is traditionally played as you look to maximize your strengths. Use your mission and your brand. Get the negotiating party to buy into your crusade, your ethos and your long-term strategy. Sell them on the benefits of being associated with your organization. Move the discussion away from the financial and focus on partnership, association, future growth and potential publicity.

For instance, we wanted the bank to lend us money at 4% interest rate. They wanted to lend us money at 6% interest rate. Rather than argue with them, we put together a proposal that involved us making some promotional videos for the bank to use, us offering some beer training and tasting to their team (thus spreading our mission!) and me speaking at one of their conferences. We also put together a document outlining the rates we could get from other banks and that we would switch banks if we did not get the deal we wanted. They then accepted our proposal at 4% interest rate and they actively wanted to do the deal. They won – they got to keep our business and got some cool perks for the staff, and video content to use for marketing, and we won – we got the finance deal in place that we needed.

Find a solution, structure and deal they feel comfortable with, and positive about. But one that is ultimately engineered around what you want.

The ability to make others passionately want to do what you want them to do is power in its purest form. It is the crack cocaine of business. A subtle coercive manipulation for the twenty-first-century business punk.

SYSTEMS DELIVER GOALS

Goals are magical things. They are like affirmations for people who are not teetering on the edge of sanity. If people don't know what they are aiming for, they don't have much chance of getting there. You need to create and curate the overall vision, get all the team to completely buy into it, then distil your vision into goals – goals for the business, goals for each department and goals for individuals. We all need a road map to guide the way.

Have goals, live them and breathe them. Share them. Write them down, graffiti them on walls, tattoo them on your butt, stare at them intently, chant them whilst in a sauna, do whatever it takes to hammer them home. Make them short-term, make them long-term, make them insanely ambitious and just out of reach. And above all make them count. Unambitious and pedestrian goals are a cruel thing to inflict on anyone, worse than being tortured by Céline Dion's singing and her thin neck.

Goals are only half of the equation. You can't just set goals and drive off into the sunset. You have to give guidance and clarity on how to achieve them. Without a path to achieving it, a goal is shallow meaningless nonsense. Give it context, direction and it will burst into life. You need to provide the vision, strategy and tools to help your team achieve your goals.

To do this, you need loads of systems – things you do on a consistent basis that boost your chances of achieving your goals in the long term. Every time you apply one of your systems you take another step towards your goals, regardless of the outcome of the specific situation.

Whatever goals you've set, you should have a list of pint-sized systems, things which you rigorously adhere to without fail, that if consistently applied will help ensure you both achieve your goals and strengthen your brand and company in the long run too. For instance, your goals for the upcoming year may be to grow turnover by 50%, increase staff engagement and take on five new premises. So, over the next twelve months you will adhere to the following systems:

- Give two heartfelt and genuine positive reinforcements to team members each day.
- Always walk away from any new deal which delivers less than 40% gross profit.
- Only look at your emails every second day.
- Ensure all new staff go through an awesome induction process.
- Always offer 30% below the asking price when bidding for new premises and never be sucked into a bidding war.
- Always ensure three massively leveraged quotes before you commit to spend over a certain amount.

Your systems will be unique to you, your own little maxims, truths and drivers. When adhered to rigorously over the long haul they will deliver success. Consistency is the key here.

For maximum impact, goals and systems need to work hand in hand. Goals are best achieved through the ruthless application of systems. You also need to detach yourself from the outcome of what you do. All you can do is make the best decision you can, implement your systems, stay true to your crusade and move towards your goals. Everything else is out of your hands.

AVOID COMMITTEE RULE

Committees are absolutely lethal, both to the now murdered fledgling concept and to the sanity of everyone involved. They are the antithesis of the creative process. A brainstorming party is for the brain-dead. Collaboration is for those with no ideas, desperately trying to magic up some half-baked nonsense from thin air. Save yourself some time and energy and disband the committee before it's formed.

Don't sacrifice your idea at the altar of committee. It will cut out its heart and burn its soul. Anything en masse bogs you down, slows you down and gets you down. Committees are breeding grounds for compromise as the tyranny of conformity rules the roost. Conformity is no place for risk and compromise is no place for innovation.

Too many cooks do spoil the broth, and at best you've reheated the obvious or at worst you've burnt something that had potential. Turn down to gas mark 2 and get out of the kitchen. You can bet your bottom dollar that if you ask some numbnuts for their opinion, they will most definitely have one. And good, bad or indifferent it will cloud your vision.

You need self-belief and integrity, and to have the courage of your convictions to run with your own ideas. Ideas are fragile; they need to be massaged until they purr. They do not need to be bastardized and overcomplicated by a meeting room full of muppets.

Like all things in life, the best ideas start small. They are born of the central vision of individuals or small and long-standing tight-knit teams, teams that are an extension of you, rather than an addition to you. Then you can fine-tune your V8 until the tailpipes sing and burn blue.

Once you have a concept tuned, locked, loaded and ready to roll you can then look to use small teams to implement and realize this vision. Individual vision is always the force behind truly remarkable ideas and concepts. And that goes across the board, from the top down and back up again.

Committees are to ideas what kryptonite is to Superman.

IDEAS ARE FRAGILE; THEY NEED TO BE MASSAGED UNTIL THEY PURR. THEY DO NOT NEED TO BE BASTARDIZED AND OVERCOMPLICATED BY A MEETING ROOM FULL OF MUPPETS.

ON MANY OCCASIONS YOU
ARE GOING TO HAVE TO BE
RUTHLESS, BRUTAL,
COLD-BLOODED AND CYNICAL.

THIS IS OK. AS LONG AS
IT IS DONE FOR THE
LONG-TERM GOOD OF WHAT
YOU ARE TRYING TO ACHIEVE.

BEING REASONABLE IS FOR AMBITIONLESS WIMPS

'The reasonable man adapts himself to the world; the unreasonable one persists in trying to adapt the world to himself. Therefore all progress depends on the unreasonable man.'
George Bernard Shaw (pre-punk iconoclast)

To grow a business you have to forget all about being reasonable. You need to thrive on being unreasonable and then have the skills to hammer your position home. You need to look after the interests of your team and business and only those interests. On many occasions you are going to have to be ruthless, brutal, cold-blooded and cynical. This is OK. As long as it is done for the long-term good of what you are trying to achieve. Think of it as a lioness eating one of her cubs to ensure the others survive. Sometimes you will have to murder your darlings.

Forget about ever taking the reasonable position, the middle road or the compromised outcome. At times you are going to have to fight tooth and nail for the outcome which is not reasonable but the outcome that represents the best possible solution for your enterprise. Making sure your business survives is going to be hella tough. Being reasonable is one way to ensure that it does not.

You need to be able to not take no for an answer. Exhaust every single angle and every single idea. Sure, you will annoy the hell out of some people. But you are far too busy to care about that. It is not about what is reasonable. It is about what is best for your business. Revel in your physical repulsion at even the notion of compromise. If you don't fight your corner, no one else will.

DON'T FOLLOW TRENDS

'I love reading fashion magazines, they show me exactly what I shouldn't be doing.'
Estée Lauder (fashion punk)

I AM A ZEITGEIST.

I WAS NOT DELIVERED INTO
THIS WORLD INTO SUBMISSION,
NOR DOES ACQUIESCENCE
RUN THROUGH MY VEINS.

I AM NOT A SHEEP WAITING TO
BE PRODDED BY MY SHEPHERD.

I AM A ZEITGEIST AND

I REFUSE TO TALK, TO WALK,

TO SLEEP WITH THE SHEEP.

THE SLAUGHTERHOUSE OF

CONFORMITY IS NOT

MY DESTINY.

I AM A ZEITGEIST.

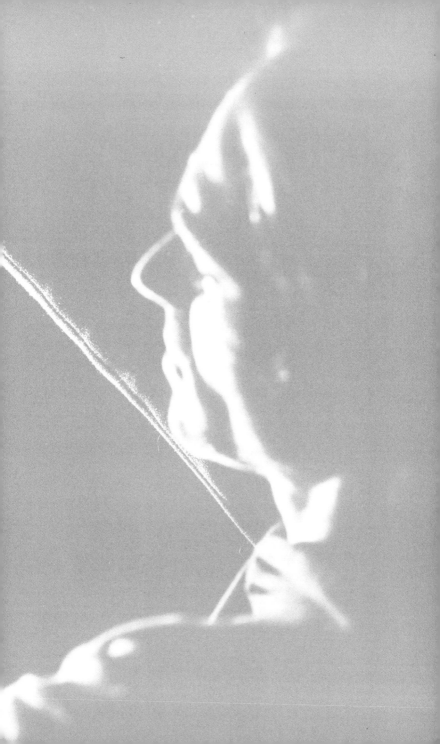

CONCLUSION:
IT IS ALL A GAME

'If you're not passionate enough from the start, you'll never stick it out.'
Steve Jobs (business punk)

Through filth, fury and originality the original old-school punks changed the world of music, and now there is the opportunity for a whole new generation of punks to change the world of business. Punk marked the dawning of the age of the individual. Now, more than ever, businesses need to be brave enough to stand out through rebellion and anarchy and have the guts to be individual too. At the heart of the punk ethos is the Dada tenet of elevating everyday things to an art form. You need to elevate everyday business things to an art form as you look to join the new wave of revolutionaries who are redefining the commercial landscape.

THE OLD-SCHOOL PUNKS LEARNED THE SKILLS THEY NEEDED TO SUCCEED.

Business is no longer about over-qualified suited bigwigs in stuffy boardrooms. It is about ordinary people having the guts and the vision to do extraordinary things. Ways of doing things have changed radically over the last few years, giving rise to a brave new world of possibilities for those bold enough to seize them.

Forget the old. Burn the establishment. Create a new world order. By following a few basic principles anyone can be a bona fide business punk.

Make damn sure your passion and your mission align, and simultaneously collide, in a flux capacitor of justification for your existence and relevance. The independent, anti-authoritarian spirit, which is punk's greatest legacy, needs to be ingrained in your entire business approach. Take a DIY approach and learn the skills you need to survive and build your own business. Don't depend on anyone for anything.

Make sure passion underpins every facet of your enterprise. Every decision must be forged with passion and purpose, edging you ever closer to achieving your crusade. And like all crusades, it will take time, and the road is long and tortuous.

Ignore advice, burn market research, laugh in the face of the naysayers and of your doubters. Mock your critics and haters. Don't live your dreams through someone else. Don't make other people's mistakes. And don't let people who don't care or don't understand influence your decisions.

Remember that being a punk does not mean not understanding your finances. The old-school punks learned the skills they needed to succeed. The best way to terrify the establishment is to make sure they know that you have the skills to beat them at their own game before making them play the game by your rules.

Put your team first. Love them, worship them, develop them and give them the confidence, skills, opportunities and resources to take on the world. And win. A company is merely the total sum of its people. Make sure your sums multiply exponentially.

Be tenacious, unwavering and true. Follow your own instincts and hold true to your course. Work hard, be passionate and enjoy the ride. Oh yeah, and don't even pretend to give a damn about what anyone else thinks.

You need to be as ruthlessly driven as you are brutally unreasonable. You need to be as passionate and selfish as you are hard-working and resolute. You need to put everything on the line for what you believe in.

Earlier in the book I told you to ignore advice. That, by default, includes all the advice in this book. So, if you were really clever you should probably just ignore the whole book. Take it, leave it, do what you want with it. Just make sure you do something.

And never forget, it is all just a game.

EARLIER IN THE BOOK
I TOLD YOU TO IGNORE ADVICE.

THAT, BY DEFAULT,
INCLUDES ALL THE ADVICE
IN THIS BOOK.